A WORSHIPER'S HEART

God Is Searching for You

Linda Patarello

God is Looking for Heart Worshipers

Unless otherwise indicated, all Scripture quotations are taken from the KJV Reference Bible. Copyright © 2000 by Zondervan. Used by permission.

Scripture quotations marked AMP are taken from the Amplified Bible.

Scripture quotations marked NIV are taken from the New International Version.

Scripture quotations marked MSG are taken from The Message Bible.

Scripture quotations marked NKJV are taken from The New King James Version.

A Worshiper's Heart (God Is Looking for You)

© 2015 by Linda Patarello

3rd Edition, © 2015, 2017, 2020

ISBN: 978-1-7360325-2-7

Editors: Daphne Parsekian, Panagiotis Gavrielatos

Published by Heaven's Treasures

PO Box 1543, Anaheim, CA 92815 www.heavenstreasures.org

Printed in the United States of America. This book or parts thereof may not be reproduced in any form, stored in a retrieval system, or transmitted in any form by any means—electronic, mechanical, photocopy, recording, or otherwise—without prior written permission from the publisher.

TABLE OF CONTENTS

CHAPTER ONE – ATTITUDE	1
CHAPTER TWO – RELATIONSHIP IS PRIORITY	8
CHAPTER THREE – QUALITY AND QUANTITY TIME	15
CHAPTER FOUR – HE'S LOOKING FOR YOU	25
CHAPTER FIVE – IT TAKES FAITH AND THANKFULNESS	32
CHAPTER SIX – WHAT IS SOAKING AND BEYOND	39
CHAPTER SEVEN – WE NEED HIS REFRESHING	46
CHAPTER EIGHT – LIVING CAN BE WORSHIP	53
CHAPTER NINE – USING YOUR IMAGINATION	60
CHAPTER TEN – WORSHIP HAS AN AROMA	67
CHAPTER ELEVEN – THE PURE IN HEART SHALL SEE GOD	74
CHAPTER TWELVE – SALVATION/BAPTISM OF THE HOLY SPIRIT	87

BIBLIOGRAPHY 93

ABOUT THE AUTHOR 94

OTHER BOOKS BY LINDA PATARELLO 96

Chapter One – Attitude

The right attitude is vital in worship. Being real and humble with the heart of a child is part of the beginnings of coming into His presence. Becoming transparent and honest with no pretenses will cause us to experience the real presence of God that we are hungering for.

Think about who you are real with and so at ease. When we are at home, this is our comfort zone.

God already knows all about you. No one can hide from God. We like our privacy and take precautions to protect it. But Almighty God the Father sees all and knows all. You could travel to the ends of the earth and run to a high mountain cave, hiding yourself from the world, and He would see every movement you made all the while.

Forget the game playing, and just come with a humble heart and give yourself to Him, showing reverence to your Loving Creator. He made you unique and who you are. So just be yourself.

> *And Jesus called a little child unto him, and set him in the midst of them. And said, Verily I say unto you, Except ye be converted, and become as little children, ye shall not enter into the kingdom of heaven. Whosoever therefore shall humble himself as this little child, the same is greatest in the kingdom of heaven.*

Matthew 18:2–4

Let's take the heart and mind of a little child. They are innocently helpless on their own. They trust someone to take care of them, to feed them, and to clothe them. Very curious and hungry to learn and be taught, they willingly try new things. A child has no cares hovering over their head that they dwell on, nor do they allow the pressures of this world to distract and paralyze them. They live in the moment, enjoying silly little games, even made up at that, pretending with vivid imaginations. This is their world. "What shall we play with next?" They only live in the present moment of the day.

This is not to say that we become foolish and irresponsible but merely that we come trusting completely, allowing your Father to take the lead since He sees ahead anyhow. Allow Him to take the wheel to the helm of your life.

> *...be clothed with humility: for God resisteth the proud, and giveth grace to the humble. Humble yourselves therefore under the mighty hand of God, that he may exalt you in due time: Casting all your care upon him; for he careth for you.*

God is Looking for Heart Worshipers

1 Peter 5:5b–7

Turn Away from Pride

We know what pride looks like. Since we have all come from the sin nature as we were born into it, we can easily identify with all the negative and fleshly ways. A child has to be taught to say yes and please. They naturally from the get go say "NO" and "I don't want to" or "I don't have to." Pride is flat out selfish, always demanding its own way. Always wanting to be seen and to be heard, first in line, picking the best and leaving behind the leftovers for others. A tantrum can come at any age, for sure, when pride is at the center of one's life. Offense will come easy and often to this type of person.

To see humility, then, just think the opposite. Putting others first and preferring them above yourself. Allowing yourself to be last and give a better seat or place in line to someone else. It's not important to be sure you have the best pick or the first pick. You let any criticism or judging comments to you just fall off like water off of a duck's back. You choose not to let it bother you and pray for them instead. You let others have the limelight, for you know that God will exalt you in due time. Demanding your way is not important. It's more important to keep peace, to build up others, and to love and bring unity. This is what pleases God.

If a person chooses to be prideful, they will not have the rich, intimate relationship with the Father. They will not take the time to listen to the Father, to Jesus, or to the Holy Spirit. Their agenda is most important. God will not talk—why should He? Why should He waste any energy on one who will not listen? That is like casting your pearls before the swine.

A man's pride shall bring him low: but honour shall uphold the humble in spirit.

Proverbs 29:23

Pride lands you flat on your face; humility prepares you for honors.

Proverbs 29:23 Message

Better it is to be of an humble spirit with the lowly, than to divide the spoil with the proud.

Proverbs 16:19

Humble yourselves [feeling very insignificant] in the presence of the Lord, and He will exalt you [He will lift you up and make your lives significant].

James 4:10 AMP

When we humble ourselves before the Lord, we are acknowledging that He is the Great One, the Mighty God who has all wisdom. You are lowering yourself. Even at times when I worship, I often literally get on the carpet and lay down on my face before God, adoring Him as Lord. This is a good thing. When you physically make yourself low to the ground, you yourself are making yourself humble. You are taking the initiative. It is much better to humble yourself and let yourself be the one doing the humbling rather than God doing the humbling for you. Remember how Satan fell? It was because of pride.

Pride goeth before destruction, and an haughty spirit before a fall.

Proverbs 16:18

When pride cometh, then cometh shame: but with the lowly is wisdom.

Proverbs 11:2

God is Looking for Heart Worshipers

Again, it is much easier to humble yourself than to have it done for you.

Jesus was humble and meek. He didn't need to flaunt His power around just to show off. He always showed His power in order to help, to heal, and to glorify the Father. We take His example for sure, and we follow His lead, for He is the perfect example. The best way to understand this is to show you the whole passage and let you see it for yourself.

1. *If there be therefore any consolation in Christ, if any comfort of love, if any fellowship of the Spirit, if any bowels and mercies,*
2. *Fulfil ye my joy, that ye be likeminded, having the same love, being of one accord, of one mind.*
3. *Let nothing be done through strife or vainglory; but in lowliness of mind let each esteem other better than themselves.*
4. *Look not every man on his own things, but every man also on the things of others.*
5. **Let this mind be in you, which was also in Christ Jesus:**
6. *Who, being in the form of God, thought it not robbery to be equal with God:*
7. *But made himself of no reputation, and took upon him the form of a servant, and was made in the likeness of men:*
8. *And being found in fashion as a man,* **he humbled himself**, *and became obedient unto death, even the death of the cross.*
9. *Wherefore God also hath highly exalted him, and given him a name which is above every name:*
10. *That at the name of Jesus every knee should bow, of things in heaven, and things in earth, and things under the earth;*
11. *And that every tongue should confess that Jesus Christ is Lord, to the glory of God the Father.*

Linda Patarello

Philippians 2:1–11

It is best to let God exalt you and not you yourself. And the very act of humbling yourself pleases God. Jesus would get away and spend much time with God in fellowship and prayer while the disciples were sleeping. He would sneak away and be alone with His Father. He always gave preference and glory to His Father. This very attitude is fitting when you come into His presence.

And I seek not mine own glory; there is one that seeketh and judgeth... Jesus answered, If I honour myself, my honour is nothing: it is my Father that honoureth me;

John 8:50,54

It is not an easy thing to humble yourself. In fact, it is one of the hardest things you can ever do. For your flesh is screaming out for attention and recognition. And the more you give in to that and feed your flesh the desires it is craving, the more you will get used to that, and it will become a habit. You will look to man for your strokes and praises. You begin to push your way through and manipulate the circumstances to get yourself in front. And selfishness grows more and more.

Let's turn it around then. Let's say you refuse to feed the flesh and realize that you have died to the flesh "in Christ"; you make yourself humble and take the back seat, not looking for man's praise. But you only want to please God and seek His praise. It is enough for you. Then God is pleased, and He exalts you in due time. In fact, He exalts you in front of many people because you chose the road of humility. Which is the better scenario then?

Come as a child, innocent and trusting God. Come and just be yourself, being honest before Him. Come humbly before your King. This is the first step to getting your attitude right in the presence of God. Of course, this is assuming you have already become saved

God is Looking for Heart Worshipers

and are hidden in Christ Jesus. He is the one that has made peace for us with God (Romans 5:1). You must always come "in Christ."

The Lord will lavish you with His attention, His love, and His praise.

He is always forgiving and merciful, seeing the best in you. The Father is always smiling down on you. When you know He loves you, you can receive correction from Him because He has your best interest at heart. He never stops working on us.

> *And I am convinced and sure of this very thing, that He Who began a good work in you will continue until the day of Jesus Christ [right up to the time of His return], developing [that good work] and perfecting and bringing it to full completion in you.*
>
> **Philippians 1:6 AMP**

Dear Father,

You are God, and I am not. You are the one who created me, and you hold the wisdom of the universe. I bow before you and humble myself. I want to be real and know you. I desire to be closer to you, and so I draw closer. You have always been here, and I receive forgiveness for thinking otherwise. I look forward to your friendship and to learning to worship you in spirit and in truth.

Chapter Two – Relationship Is Priority

I remember a conversation I had with a man who was in his 60s.

He said when he was single, he and his roommates were so hungry for God. They would spend much time seeking God in prayer and worship and in the Word. Every night they would take turns preaching and teaching the Bible study. He said he easily spent five hours a day in prayer and seeking God. They began to see miracles, and the power of God became so strong that he didn't even have to lay hands on a person. His mere presence in the room would bring healing. He became so busy ministering and doing the work of the kingdom that the years went by, and all of a sudden, gone were the days of seeking God. By the time I met up with him and we were having our conversation, he was struggling to get back to God. Oh, he was still a Christian, and he loved God and all. But that sweet and intimate relationship seemed to fall by the wayside. He told me, "Please learn from my mistake; always stay close to God. He is your first priority, even above ministry."

Stay Connected to the Vine

Without relationship and being in the presence of God on a regular basis, you will simply dry up. It's exactly like John 15 explains. We must be connected to the vine, always, or we will wither up and die.

Our power and life come from Him, and being connected to Him.

He is our everything. Our inner strength, all power, all joy, all love, and on and on flow out from Him. He is like the sap of life that flows through the trees from the deep embedded roots to the far reaching branches of bushy leaves. No sap, no life. Once we have accepted Christ, we are one. We are in union with Him. We are "in Christ." Our spirit is one with God's Spirit. But if you are ignorant about that fact, you will not get to enjoy the benefits of it. Realizing and believing that we are one with Him is the key. But life can get busy, and we can forget our oneness with Jesus. We begin to function on our own, making our own decisions and choices. And before you know it, you have drifted off. When you are regularly in His presence, you will constantly keep the right perspective of who is Lord, and who is the Good Shepherd, and that we are only the sheep. Our life's plan comes from His hand. The power and anointing and the fullness of joy come from Him and only Him.

And so as we continually come to sit at the Lord's feet, seeking His great and ancient wisdom, even sitting in His presence without a word on either side, it will be overwhelmingly comforting and strengthening. His presence will center you and will put you back into the perfect balance of life. You will learn to cast your cares on Him there and receive of His blissful peace.

We crave closeness. God made us this way. As human beings, we function best when we have healthy and happy relationships, where there is peace, laughter, and hugs. Being a parent, I can remember the joy of holding my babies close to me. I wanted them to feel the security and the warmth of my touch. Sometimes when they were tiny, I enjoyed letting them take a nap on my chest, and I could hear their small breathing. They could hear my constant heartbeat. I know it was a comfort to them. Parents love to comfort their children. Why wouldn't God be any different? After all, our good desires came from Him. We were made in His image. We are His children,

Relationship Is Priority

and He loves to comfort us. A good parent always loves to spend time with their kids, no matter what the age.

A Missionary Example

There was a missionary named Frank Laubach, who wrote a book called *Letters by a Modern Mystic*. This book was first published in 1937. He was a lonely missionary serving on the island of Mindanao in the Philippines and was a Protestant among many Muslims. He journaled to God and shared his letters in this great book. He set out to do an experiment, and each day he would practice the presence of God as he journaled this experience. There were times he would write and allow the Spirit of God to write through him. There were such intimate accounts of His conversations with God. He got to the point where it was so lonely and quiet from human contact, yet God's company became so rich and meaningful. He practiced acknowledging the presence of God so much that he could sense Him wherever he was.

Linda Patarello

This is possible for us as well, but we must begin to seek Him by faith.

I have since begun to keep my journal in a different way. I will write my entries and recall my day or my experiences. And then I will say, "Okay, Holy Spirit, it's your turn to speak." I don't think or analyze the next sentences; I just start writing what comes to mind. And as long as you are judging everything according to the Scriptures, what will come out will be very encouraging. I have discovered much wisdom and reassurance this way. It always lines up with His Word.
He will never speak against His Word or contradict it.

When the weather is right, I prefer to spend much time outside in the wonders of God's creation. As I am working in the garden, digging out the carrots and smelling the pungent basil as I rub it with my hands, I think of how He decided to put fragrances into the plants and flowers He created. He knew we would like this. I hear His voice from inside my heart more clear as I am playing in the garden that He made for me. His wisdom encourages me as I listen to His reasoning of the hows and whys of His making plants and seeds. He will give me parallels of life. Sometimes you need not say one word to each other. Just to be in His presence is nurturing. You enjoy the earth together. I can look up at the clouds slowly rolling by, and I know all of this was made for me to enjoy and that it gives Him great pleasure watching me enjoy it all. The Father has great patience with us as we learn. He allows us to come along at our own speed. He doesn't push or control us angrily as the enemy does. He is a gentle, loving Father who waits for us to come, who longs for us to seek Him.

I will share with you some of my own journal entries to the Lord and His responses:

Feb. 2, 2014

God is Looking for Heart Worshipers

Father, thank you for teaching me new things. Avenues I have never gone before in ministry. (I was going through a season of learning how to use software to record songs for Him that He had given me. I could not understand this software before, but the Holy Spirit began to give me understanding, for it was the right season.) Thank you for helping me each step of the way—it's working Lord! I am having so much fun….

"I'm pleased with you. I'm pleased with your leap of faith in branching out and trying new things. I love when my kids take a risk and dare to believe. When they dare to try something they've never done. If you dare, I dare to help and bless it. According to your faith, be it done unto you. If you have simple faith, then you get simple answers. If you have water

Relationship Is Priority

walking faith, then you will walk on the water. You were made to do so. My children were made in my image. It is surely a natural thing. I should expect no less. Reach higher, reach further, think bigger, see the impossible. Expand your vision for more. This is where I want you to live, speak, and stay—out on a limb, where I can catch you!

Feb. 6, 2014

Lord, speak to me regarding this season of my life and into the next. I want to follow your lead. I don't want to veer off the path you have set for me….

"I trim the branches and tend to your growth, your direction. I direct your steps, right into the plan that I have made for you. I direct you to the right doors and the right people in the right season. Yours is to follow, to be pliable, to let me lead. Not to question but to trust me. As you dream, I develop the plan in you, allowing you to see parts of it. The more you yield to me, the faster we get there. As you give me full control, I will steer you. As you take control, you have a tendency to veer off the path. But if you will find your satisfaction in me instead of people, positions, things, or fame, you will keep free of the temptations, distractions, detours, and pitfalls.

Saint Augustine said, "Thou hast made us for Thyself, and our souls are restless until they find their rest in Thee."

No one can give us the highest satisfaction in a relationship but God. Whether you are taking time to talk to your Abba Father God, for sometimes we just need the loving protection of our Father and His heart is full of love for you and me, or you are talking with Jesus, who is your bridegroom, your brother, your friend, your Master, and your Savior, who has rescued you from the pit and has provided all the grace you need in this life and into the next. You may be learning to speak with the Holy Spirit, who is your helper, your guide, and your comforter. He will teach you all things and help you remember the words of Jesus. They are one, yet they each have their own personalities. They are your real family. Get to know them.

This verse is a nice description of each one's role.

> *The grace of the Lord Jesus Christ, and the love of God, and the communion of the Holy Spirit be with you all. Amen.*
>
> **2 Corinthians 13:14 NKJV**

Grace comes from and because of Jesus. All that we have is because of Jesus and His cross. Love comes from God because God is Love. The fellowship and communion come from the Holy Spirit.

God is Looking for Heart Worshipers

Ministry must never take the place of a relationship with God. Ministry will come out of your relationship with God. It will be a joy to serve Him in ministry because of your great love for Him. But you must make every effort to guard and protect your friendship, your intimacy, and your time with Him.

Linda Patarello

Chapter Three – Quality and Quantity Time

My friend Jeffrey said it so perfectly. When a mom puts her baby in the church nursery on a Sunday morning and happily comes back to pick her child up among all the busy sounds of babies crying, laughing, and gurgling, she can spot which sound belongs to her precious baby. This is because of the time spent with her child, day in and day out. We know our family's voices.

When you spend so much time with the Lord, the same will happen. And so it is in the opposite way. When a person listens so much to the evil one, they know his voice. You could be doing that unknowingly even. When a person worries or stays in fear or strife, they can focus their attention on these kind of thoughts. You could say you park your mind here, you are camping out here, thinking and dwelling on worry. Who do you think brings many of these thoughts your way? Maybe you, maybe the enemy. But these thoughts do not come from God. When you willingly entertain these thoughts, the devil and his demons will gladly feed you more; while you are imagining the worst, you are listening to him and getting to know that voice. We must decide and choose to close that door to all those negative thoughts and listen to God's Word and think and feed on His Word, which is His voice. The more you know God's Word, the more you open the way to hearing His voice because He speaks through His Word. As you spend time with Him, you will get used to His voice.

I believe that abundant life flows from this place called "Relationship." Even in the natural, when you have a great relationship, you have such contentment and satisfaction. Life seems right, and there is happiness and security. When you have a broken relationship, there is little to no communication, and there is hurt, sadness, and loneliness. Why do we think we can have a thriving Christian walk without a close relationship with our Creator, who is our real family?

> *And call no man your father upon the earth: for one is your Father, which is in heaven.*
> **Matthew 23:9**

God really is your Father. And Jesus really is your brother. The Holy Trinity is your real family. Get used to this thought. Think about it often. There are times I tell the Lord, "You are my family." How much closer can we get to God the Father than just realizing that He is your real Father who made you, who made every member and part of your body.

Just because we don't see Him right now doesn't mean we can't spend time with Him, talking and listening, carrying on good conversations. Why not? Wherever you go, He goes too. Whatever you think, He sees that too. He is nearer than your spouse. He is a very part of you, one with you.

Therefore if any man be in Christ…

2 Corinthians 5:17

A Few Tips on Worship

I believe in the beginning, and really even later, it is good to set aside private time to spend with Him and a private place, where there are no distractions. Even now I do this. Think of it. If you have a very special relationship that you treasure, aren't there times that you want them all to yourself, where you set aside times where you will not be bothered? To know the Lord is to have a very special relationship indeed. This is a royal relationship with the King. You may have to make time in the early morning or late at night. But this is something you have to take responsibility for. No one can do this for you. We must guard this time. Just like we guard our thoughts, we must guard our quiet time with Jesus.

So let's say you come to that special time…now what? Sometimes it may take a while to get rid of distractions and thoughts that preoccupy you. You keep working on it till you have disciplined yourself. There are times I may put on some soft worship music to help me focus my mind on Him. There is no right or perfect way. There is no law that you have to do it a certain way.

For me now, there are times when I play my guitar and sing. But then there are many times when I just sing on my own with nothing. All you need is your voice, and He sees your heart. If your heart is sincere, that is what matters, not how professional you sound or off key you may be. I may open the Bible to the psalms or a favorite passage and sing to Him from that. I may go straight to getting on my face before God and just keeping quiet. I picture myself in His throne room and lay prostrate before Him. I use my imagination that is from God, and I picture the angels worshipping. I picture how breathtakingly beautiful God must look, full of majesty and light.

Honour and majesty are before him: strength and beauty are in his sanctuary.

Psalm 96:6

I may whisper, "I worship you Lord; I humble myself before you. I come to put my mind on you, not ask for anything. I only want to be with you and worship you alone."

I tell Him that I love Him and thank Him for all He has done for me.

During these times, I turn down my cellphone and put it somewhere else, even in another room. I do not want to be disturbed. If you are able, schedule a span of time where you are not conscious of it. Even a few hours is good and can go quickly. This part is really all according to how hungry you are for His presence. If you are looking at your watch, well, that will tell you where your heart is. I don't mean to put a guilt trip on you. But a person either wants more of God or not. Yes you can change if you so desire. If that is the case, then you push through this time until the desire grows. It can grow. It did for me. I honestly used to look at the clock. "I really need to make this quick, because I have errands I need to do."

God will meet you where you are at. If you want a little, you will get a little. If you have a huge appetite for God, you will be filled. According to your faith be it done unto you.

Draw nigh to God, and he will draw nigh to you.

James 4:8

Linda Patarello

Mary Magdalene, a True Worshipper

I want to share with you a story in the Bible that explains what I am talking about. As you meditate on it more and more, I believe the Holy Spirit will reveal it to you. This is a beautiful passage of the resurrection and love, passion, and worship from two of the followers of Jesus, John and Mary Magdalene.

Jesus was buried. And that's pretty much all the disciples saw. They became afraid and were hiding out. So we begin at verse 1 of John 20:

> *The first day of the week cometh Mary Magdalene (Magdalene in the Greek is "Tower") early, when it was yet dark, unto the sepulchre, and seeth the stone taken away from the sepulchre.*

There are different accounts in the other gospels in which other ladies came too; maybe they could have come separate and met Mary. But this says here in verses 2–18 that she was alone.

> *Then she runneth, and cometh to Simon Peter,* **and the other disciple, whom Jesus loved,** *and saith unto them, They have taken away the LORD out of the sepulchre, and we know not where they have laid Him. Peter therefore went forth, and that other disciple, and came to the sepulchre. So they ran both together:* **and the other disciple did outrun Peter, and came first to the sepulchre. And he stooping down, and looking in, saw the linen clothes lying; yet went he not in.** *Then cometh Simon Peter following him, and went into the sepulchre, and seeth the linen clothes lie, and the napkin that was about his head, not lying with linen clothes, but wrapped together in a place by itself.*
>
> *Vs 8* **then went in also that other disciple, which came first to the sepulchre, and he saw and believed.** *For*

as yet they knew not the scripture, that he must rise again from the dead. Then the disciples went away again unto their own home.

But Mary stood without at the sepulchre weeping: and as she wept, she stooped down, and looked into the sepulchre. And seeth two angels in white sitting, the one at the head, and the other at the feet, where the body of Jesus had lain. And they say unto her, Woman, why weepest thou? She saith unto them, Because they have taken away my LORD, and I know not where they have laid Him. And when she had thus said, she turned herself back, and saw Jesus standing, and knew not that it was Jesus. Jesus saith unto her, Woman, Why weepest thou? whom seekest thou? She, supposing him to be the gardener, saith unto him, Sir, if thou have borne him hence, tell me where thou hast laid him, and I will take him away.

Jesus saith unto her, Mary. She turned herself, and saith unto him, Rabboni; which is to say, Master.

Jesus saith unto her, Touch me not; for I am not yet ascended to my Father: but go to my brethren, and say unto them, I ascend unto my Father, and your Father; and to my God and to your God.

Mary Magdalene came and told the disciples that she had seen the LORD, and that He had spoken these things unto her.

Let's first look at John. We believe that John is writing this, for it is the book of the Gospel of John. He doesn't mention his own name, but what is mentioned is "the other disciple, whom Jesus loved."

Now there was leaning on Jesus' bosom one of his disciples, whom Jesus loved.

Linda Patarello

John 13:23

Jesus loved them all. But maybe some more than others had the revelation of that deep love. Maybe they were like David, a man after God's heart.

Now, reading the above account in John chapter 20, we find that when John heard what Mary Magdalene had said, he ran to the tomb with Peter, but he overtook Peter, which to me shows his passion. And when they got to the tomb, Peter went right in, but John stooped at the sepulcher and did not go in at first. There was a humility, I believe, a reverence, a waiting. And verse 8 says that when he saw the linen clothes lying there, he believed. It doesn't say yet that Peter believed.

There are some that will be hungrier than others. But if one wants it and isn't hungry yet, that also can change. It comes by immersing yourself in His Word and making His Word your home, your comfort zone. The hunger for more steadily grows. The more a person hangs around a brook and puts their feet in, well, it's just a matter of time before you are swimming in the deep waters. When you spend time watching a lot of television, after a while, it becomes your comfort zone. You know what shows are on at what time. Some of those shows become your favorites, and then you begin to plan your life and evening activities around those very shows. When I was a kid, they were somewhat wholesome, but today they are downright dangerous for your soul. *To be carnally minded is death; but to be spiritually minded is life and peace* (Romans 8:6). If you are going to put waste in your mind, just expect a slow death. Before you even realize it, darkness will overcome you in every area of your life. I'm very serious about this. It's time we guard our hearts and our minds, along with our eyes. I give my whole life to God, and His Word brings me life and peace.

God is Looking for Heart Worshipers

Now let's look at Mary. As I meditated on this chapter, so many things began to unravel. The Holy Spirit reveals the wisdom of the Scriptures to us as we meditate. The name Mary speaks of *"rebelliousness"* in the Greek.

She was a sinner, and a good one, but since she came to believe in Jesus, she was strong in God's kingdom. She was now rebellious toward the kingdom of darkness. You can be born with a strong will, but if you're pointed in the right direction, you can be a strong leader for good.

There are different accounts in the gospels about this true story. In Luke 24 it speaks of several ladies going to the tomb early in the morning as well as in Mark 16 and Matthew 28. But it was Mary whom Jesus first appeared and spoke to (Mark 16:9). But let us look at the account of John 20. She came early, in the dark, then ran back after she saw the stone gone. She hadn't gone in yet. She ran to tell Peter and John. She then came with the disciples, still staying outside. When they left, she was the one that stayed outside weeping. It says she stooped down and looked in. She saw two angels sitting, dressed in white. Now, if they were sitting, wouldn't they maybe have been there when Peter and John were there? Why did only Mary then see them and even hear them speak to her? I don't know; it doesn't say. We can only guess, and when we get to heaven, we will know all the hows and whys of the resurrection. Was it because she stayed? Because she loved Him so? God allowed Mary to hear the angels speak even. Usually when people see angels, the Bible says that they were afraid. Maybe she didn't know they were angels. They asked her why she was crying. She really thought someone came to take Him away; she didn't understand about the resurrection. She turned around and saw Jesus standing, whom she thought was the gardener. He even asked why she was crying. Didn't she know that this was a tremendous day of victory? When the disciples were there, was
Jesus invisible, watching them, maybe even from outside? Finally

Linda Patarello

Jesus called her by name: "Mary."

Can you imagine Jesus calling you by name? He knows your name. She knew that voice then, the way He said her name. I would melt if He called my name. He uncovered his identity when He said her name. The Bible says she turned herself and said, "Rabboni," which means "Master." In an instant she must have grabbed onto Him or thrown herself at his feet and held onto Him. I believe this tells us that Jesus was so approachable that He welcomed all people, from children to adults, to Himself. They felt His mercy, His acceptance, and His love. Those that wanted His love and chose to believe in Him felt comfortable with Him. Jesus had to tell her "Touch me not." Other translations say, "Stop clinging to me," or "Don't cling to me."

> *For I am not yet ascended to my Father: but go to my brethren, and say unto them, I ascend unto my Father, and your Father; and to my God, and your God.*
>
> **John 20:17**

For He was telling the truth. Because of the cross and the resurrection, God was truly now our God and our Father. Jesus made it so! I often wonder, why did He show Himself before He went to His Father? I would like to ask Jesus that question one day. If the disciples had stayed, would they have seen Him? So many questions. Is it the more we hunger, the more we are fed? I do believe so.

> *Draw nigh to God, and he will draw nigh to you. Cleanse your hands ye sinners; and purify your hearts, ye double minded.*
>
> **James 4:8**

> *Blessed are they which do hunger and thirst after righteousness: for they shall be filled.*
>
> **Matthew 5:6**

God is Looking for Heart Worshipers

Blessed are the pure in heart: for they shall see God.

Matthew 5:8

They all ended up seeing Him, but Mary got to see Him first. She came and told the disciples what she had seen and that He spoke these things to her. I bet Peter and John could have kicked themselves for leaving. They must have all quizzed her all afternoon: "What did he look like? How did he seem? Tell us again, did he mention us?" Now on the same day, the Bible says that they were all together.

Picture it:

Then the same day at evening, being the first day of the week, when the doors were shut where the disciples were assembled for fear of the Jews, came Jesus and stood in the midst, and saith unto them, Peace be unto you. And when he had so said, he showed unto them his hands and his side. Then were the disciples glad, when they saw the LORD.

John 20:19–20

What a wonderful story and example of having passion for Jesus.

Chapter Four – He's Looking for You

To Worship Him in Spirit and in Truth

I wonder how the Father feels; while He wants such a close relationship with His children, in ignorance, they come to him begging and trying to experience Him with their feelings? Does He shake His head when they come and shake their fist at Him, saying, "Why don't you show yourself to me!" Does He think, *Oh, how I wish they would just believe my Word and come to me believing what I already have told them, that I already have proved to them my love.* It must be so refreshing to Him when one of His own comes along and says, "Father, I want to spend time with you today and just simply be with you, enjoying your presence."

Do you want a clearer example? All right, let's take child A and child B. You can imagine and make them to be whatever age you would like. We can even make them women since that is what I am.

Child A: (wants to feel God—she says this will help her to believe)

She has an evening with no plans set, and so she is excited to spend that time to seek God. Someone told her that she could hear God's voice. She turns off the phone, gets out her Bible, and begins to pray. "Okay, God, I'm ready now; I'm listening." She waits for a goose bump feeling. Then she looks around to see if any glory will appear. Nothing happens. She begins to question that maybe she should have fasted or prayed longer. "Where is He? They said I would hear His voice. Maybe God loves them more. This is not working for me."

Child B: (Takes God at His Word, even though she has never seen Him)

She has an evening with no plans set, and so she is excited to spend that time to see God. She believes His Word, and she utterly trusts Him even though she cannot see or feel Him. "Father, Your Word says in Hebrews 13:5 that you will never leave me or forsake me, so therefore I believe you are here. I believe you are listening to me and that you see me. Your ears are open to my cry, as your Word says. And so I will enjoy your presence now. I want to say that I love you, heavenly Father. I want to say it from my heart that I trust you and thank you for your promises to me."

Which child of God do you think pleased God more? He loves both. But He is pleased when His children trust Him for who He says He is and what He says He can do.

Let's take a look at a passage in the Wuest Translation:

> **John 4:23–24**: *But there comes an hour and it is now, when the genuine worshippers shall worship the Father in a spiritual sphere, and in the sphere of truth. For indeed, the Father is*

God is Looking for Heart Worshipers

seeking such as these who worship Him. God as to His nature is spirit, and for those who are worshipping, it is necessary in the nature of the case to be worshipping in a spiritual sphere, and in the sphere of truth.

KJV: But the hour cometh, and now is, when the <u>true worshippers</u> shall <u>worship</u> the Father in <u>spirit</u> and in <u>truth</u>: for the Father <u>seeketh</u> such to <u>worship</u> Him. God is a spirit: and they that <u>worship</u> him must <u>worship</u> him in <u>spirit</u> and in <u>truth</u>.

He Is Looking for You

The first Greek word we can research is "Worship" (*Proskyneo*). This means to kiss the hand in token of reverence or to prostrate oneself in reverence. To lay prostrate is this: to actually lay down on the ground to worship. We are not used to seeing this at all. The most common thing we usually see in worship is when someone raises their hands. But God is actually looking for believers to come to the point where they want Him so much, love Him so much, that they will gladly lay down on the ground to worship Him, giving their whole life to Him.

This same word, Proskyneo, is used when the wise men came to worship Jesus in Matthew 2:2 as well as in Matthew 4:10, when the devil tempted Jesus to worship him. He wanted Jesus to lay down and to kiss his hand. In Revelation 4:10, the 24 elders fall down before Him who is on the throne and worship Him. We will be doing this in heaven!

When the verse says "true worshippers," it is speaking of genuine. "True" in the Greek is *Alethinos*. What I first think of is when I see real leather and it is stamped "Genuine Leather." There is only real; anything else is fake leather that may feel like the real thing, but it's not. There is only one real kind. The same here. Alethinos is speaking of the opposite of counterfeit, which means there is a counterfeit to a true worshipper.

Linda Patarello

In Spirit and in Truth

Next we look at "spirit and in truth." This has always been sort of hazy to me. What does that mean, spirit and in truth? Spirit is originally from the root Greek word *"Pneo,"* which means "to breath, to blow, of the wind."

But this word is *Pneuma*, a movement of air, a blast. It also speaks of the Holy Spirit. So to worship in spirit is to worship Him in His realm. For He is a spirit. We are a spirit. And if we are of His, then He is in us and we are one. We must worship in His realm. In actuality, this also is our realm, for we are in the spirit because we are new creations. We are a royal priesthood because Jesus has made us to be that because of His grace.

So we begin with a decision to worship regardless of what we feel, and then we do something that shows we are worshipping with our bodies.

We will lift up our hands, and we can kneel and lie prostrate with our physical bodies; we do this by faith. It is an act of faith and sacrifice. I believe this is where we use everything. Our imagination, will, and mind focus in on Him and His throne. Our body moves to worship. We are not looking at anyone else, not concerned about anyone but Him. He is the focus of our attention. I do believe if you are filled with the Holy Spirit and speaking in tongues, you will have the most meaningful worship that He has intended for you. Remember in Acts 1 and 2? Jesus told the disciples in Acts 1:5, *"...but you shall be baptized with the Holy Spirit not many days from now"* (NKJV).

When the Holy Spirit fills you and comes to live in you, it is forever. Acts 1:8 says, *"But you shall receive power when the Holy Spirit has come upon you; and you shall be witnesses to me in Jerusalem, and in the all Judea and Samaria, and to the end of the earth"* (NKJV).

God is Looking for Heart Worshipers

When the Day of Pentecost had fully come, they were all with one accord in one place. And suddenly, as of a rushing mighty wind, and it filled the whole house where they were sitting. Then there appeared to them divided tongues, as of fire, and one sat upon each of them. And they were all filled with the Holy Spirit and began to speak with other tongues, as the Spirit gave them utterance.

Acts 2:1–4 NKJV

He Is Looking for You

So we are to worship the Lord in the realm of the Spirit. This is to be coupled with the "Truth." The Greek word here is *"Aletheia."* In truth, verity. I believe this is speaking of God's Word. God's Word is truth. It is stable. There are three accounts in the gospels where the same verse is stated: **Matthew 24:35, Mark 13:31**, and **Luke 21:33**.

Heaven and earth shall pass away, but my words shall not pass away.

Jesus said in **John 17:17**, *"Sanctify them by Your truth. Your word is truth"* (NKJV).

God's Word never changes. So we are to worship Him according to His Word, not by our feelings. This means we must know His Word. Yes, it is a matter of life and death—not when it is convenient for you. It should not even be a passing hobby. The Word of God is our life. It is full of power and is alive. It is able to change us and make us more like Him.

The last word we will look at is seeketh, Zeteo. It is a verb—to be seeking; to seek in order to find; to desire. He is looking and still looking for people to worship Him in Spirit and in truth. He is looking for you. He is looking for genuine worshippers, not for those that just want to pay their obligation and go to church on

Sunday just to say they went to church on Sunday. A genuine worshipper is someone who is hungry for Him. Nothing and no one else will do. They must have more of Him. The hunger does not subside; it only continues and grows stronger. It will not be quenched until they have experienced more and more of Him by spending time with Him. We can have all we want now, thank God, because of Jesus. The veil was torn down by God Himself when Jesus died on the cross. *And Jesus cried out with a loud voice, and breathed His last. Then the veil of the temple was torn in two from top to bottom* (Mark 15:37–38). This veil was thick. Josephus reported that the veil was four inches thick, that it was renewed every year, and that horses tied to each side could not pull it apart. It barred all but the high priest from the presence of God, but when it was torn in two at the death of Jesus of Nazareth, access to God was made available to all who come through Him.

No one could have torn it, much less from the top to the bottom. God wanted us to come to Him, and now we can. Jesus has made peace for us to come to God.

> *Therefore, having been justified by faith, we have peace with God through our Lord Jesus Christ, through whom also we have access by faith into this grace in which we stand, and rejoice in hope of the glory of God.*
> **Romans 5:1–2 NKJV**

You see, God is not hiding from you! He is looking for you! Come to Him!

Dear Lord,

To think that you made the way for me to come to you. Your arms have been open wide for me. You have been waiting for me all along and looking forward to having me as your child. You wanted to adopt me as your child. I come freely and willingly. Thank you for loving me.

Chapter Five – It Takes Faith and Thankfulness

The scripture that always comes to mind is **Hebrews 10:38**—

The just shall live by faith—and also **2 Corinthians 5:7**: *For we walk by faith, not by sight.*

We are born in a physical world, and as we grow up, we become accustomed to completely using our five senses. We have not known any other way. We feel sad, so we cry, and when we feel happy, we laugh. When we hear of violent news or a loud screeching sound, we get scared. If we can see it, then we will believe it. This may have been so much of our lives, but in God's kingdom, once you become a believer, things must change. If God is a Spirit and He lives by faith, then doesn't it make sense that that is what we need to do? Especially when He then gives us the command to live by faith. He wants us to walk by faith, not by sight any longer. It may seem backwards to you, but we have been backwards all along because of the sin of Adam. His sin brought about the sin nature to the whole world.

Every person is born into sin on this earth because of Adam.

> *Wherefore, as by one man sin entered into the world, and death by sin; and so death passed upon all men, for that all have sinned:*

Romans 5:12

So when we realize that we are in a new kingdom, we must learn the new laws of the kingdom. And one of them is faith. It is now faith that moves us and not our feelings or our senses. We refuse to let our feelings dictate our actions or our choices.

I'm not going to look at the natural anymore, at what I see. God my Father teaches me through His Word this new way. A child follows what His Father does. So how does God do it?

> *...even God, who quickeneth the dead, and calleth those things which be not as though they were.*

Romans 4:17

He speaks to death and the things that are not; He calls them as though they were. He doesn't care if something is not there. He calls it into being. He acts like it's so. His faith moves things and circumstances. He doesn't let them move Him. He is in charge. Well, guess what? We are supposed to do the same thing as our Father.

So how do we apply this to worship? I hear so many say, "I know about faith. Yes, of course, I've heard all this before. I've heard these scriptures a gazillion times." Yet when it comes to worship, some of these same people are wondering where God is. Why can't they see or feel Him?

If we look for a feeling, we are going to miss it! You must apply the word of God to worship. Because God said in His Word ...*for he hath said, I will never leave thee, nor forsake thee* (**Hebrews 13:5b**).

You must believe it, period. So when you come in worship, whether you see a sign or a feather or a ray of light, it doesn't matter. You can worship Him anyways, believing His word. Whether you feel the fire, or the wind rushing into the room, or the electricity in your body, it doesn't matter; you simply believe that He is there because His Word said so.

It Takes Faith and Thankfulness

I can't tell you how many times that I worshipped, and still it happens at times, when I don't feel a darn thing. I don't see anything. All I have to lean on and to base my worship on is His Word, the end. But you know what? That is good enough. *While I live will I praise the Lord: I will sing praises unto my God while I have any being* (**Psalm 146:2**). Keep pressing on, my friend.

For you are pleasing the Living God! He is watching you diligently!

> ***But without faith it is impossible to please him:*** *for he that cometh to God must believe that he is, and that he is a rewarder of them that **diligently seek him**.*
> **Hebrews 11:6**

There are only two ways: coming in faith or not coming in faith. And if you are not coming in faith, well then, it's probably because you are coming in feeling. And if you are coming looking for Him through a feeling, the above verse explains that you are not pleasing

Him; in fact, it is impossible to please Him. You have to come in the kingdom way, which is faith. It is the key that unlocks the door. Even a child can do this. They will be better at it than an adult. For it is simple trust. "God said it, I believe it, let's go."

So let's say you decide to come in faith and forget about feeling His presence; a few things will take place:

You will be pleasing God, and you will make Him happy.

- If you get into this habit and press on, you will be diligently seeking Him.
- He rewards those that diligently seek Him.
- You will learn how to come into His realm.
- You are putting yourself in the right posture to listen to God.
- You are getting the right perspective again, humbling yourself and remembering who is Lord.
- You are forgetting about the problems and the things of this world.
- You will be refreshed and full of peace, renewed by His love.
- You are entering into eternity, where God is, where you are welcome.

The word "diligently" in **Hebrews 11:6** in the Greek is "ekzeteo," which is a verb. It means to seek out and to search for. It can also mean to investigate. If you just come once or twice and don't see anything happening, that is not seeking diligently. That is only trying it out. God doesn't want you to just try Him out. He is looking for those that really want a relationship with Him. He is looking for those who have a hunger that is not going to be filled until they are satisfied with His presence and only His presence.

Let's read this same verse in the Wuest translation, which is great to see the closest capturing of the Greek:

> *Now, without faith it is impossible to please Him at all. For he who comes to God must of the necessity in the nature of the case believe that He exists, that He also becomes a rewarder of those who diligently seek Him out.*

Hebrews 11:6 Wuest

Faith is His realm. He is a faith God. You must come to Him in faith. There is no other way. And so the way of faith is the only way to really worship the living God. Here is a prayer example I would give you that I have done as I come to the Lord by faith to worship:

It Takes Faith and Thankfulness

Father, I come to you to worship you today. I believe your Word. I trust you. I may not see you or feel you right now, but that is okay. I still believe you. I thank you for your many blessings to me. I thank you for your mercy and your love. You are a good God, a great Father. I worship you for who you are and for your holiness. Your word says "Let everything that has breath praise you." Well, I have breath. And it is right to give you praise. It is good to honor you with my lips. From my heart, Lord, I want to tell you that I love you. I come close to you to say I love you. I thank you that you hear me and that you see me. I'm so glad that at this very moment, I'm making you happy.

If you make a habit of coming to the Father, to Jesus, to the Holy Spirit, by faith in worship like this, there will come times when you physically will sense His glory, His presence. You can do nothing but cry and laugh at the same time. Where in the natural you may still be on your knees in your bedroom, in the spirit, you know that you are before His throne. He will reward you. But the key that unlocks the door is faith.

Linda Patarello

Thankfulness

This is the language of heaven. I don't see gripers and complainers in heaven. Negativity looks at the problem. You cannot praise God in this state, and there is no faith in this state. Thankfulness takes faith.

Praise takes faith, regardless of what you may be going through.

I remember going through divorce and foreclosure at the same time, and the Lord spoke to me to get strong in His Word. He told me I was free to stay in depression and a pity party if I wanted to but that only I could change my attitude. He couldn't even do it for me. I had to do it, for it was my mind, my freewill, not His. So in those days, I began to meditate on the love of God, any scriptures that spoke on the love of God for me. I took seriously what He said, that only I could do this. Only I could make me happy. I knew my depressing, negative thoughts had to go and that I had the freedom to think on what I wanted. Only His Word could change things as I gave myself to it in the same way I used to give myself to the dark thoughts of fear.

I spent a lot of alone time in those days, thinking on His Word and worshipping Him. I sang to Him in tears as He was healing my heart with His great love. I made myself be thankful. Yes, you can make yourself be thankful. You alone have to do this. And if you mess up and think a negative thought, well, repent and go back to the praise and thankfulness. It's a new way that you are developing. I pressed on and began to see a change in a few months. As I used to read the Bible, I never realized how positive it was. It is so positive! Which means God and heaven's kingdom is positive. This means that we are to look at the answer, not the problem. We are free to choose. Today you can be thankful if you like, tomorrow as well if you so choose.

God is Looking for Heart Worshipers

Here are a few scriptures that will encourage you:

*Enter into his gates with thanksgiving, and into his courts with praise: be **thankful** unto him, and bless his name.*

Psalm 100:4

*Because that, when they knew God, they glorified him not as God, neither were **thankful**; but became vain in their imaginations, and their foolish heart was darkened.*

Romans 1:21

*And let the peace of God rule in your hearts, to the which also ye are called in one body; and be ye **thankful**.*

Colossians 3:15

Chapter Six – What Is Soaking and Beyond

Although this word isn't in the Bible, the word "soaking" is becoming more and more well known. But even if we never used this term, that would be fine, because there are many good scriptures that we could use to explain this same term "soaking." Since it is getting to be more popular, I would like to explain my version of it and, more importantly, let us look and lean on the scriptures.

If you were to take a dry sponge and hold it in your hand, it would be rough and dry. It wouldn't be holding anything. But what is the purpose of a sponge? To hold liquid, mainly used for holding water. If you place a dry sponge in a bowl of water for a while, the water will saturate into the sponge. When people speak of soaking in God's presence, what they mean is, they are saturating themselves with the presence of God. But in order to do that, you must stay awhile. So the word "soaking" really means to me "to stay awhile." From Merriam Webster Dictionary—Soak: to put (something) in a liquid for a period of time: to take a long bath: to make (someone or something) very wet with water or another liquid.

Full Definition:

1: to lie immersed in liquid (as water): become saturated by or as if by immersion

2a: to enter or pass through something by or as if by pores or interstices: <u>permeate</u>

2b: to penetrate or affect the mind or feelings—usually used with in or into

Even the disciples waited in the upper room on the day of Pentecost.
Jesus told them to wait.

> *And, behold, I send the promise of my Father upon you: but tarry ye in the city of Jerusalem, until ye be endued with power from on high.*
> **Luke 24:49**

> *And when the day of Pentecost was fully come, they were all with one accord in one place. And suddenly there came a sound from heaven as of a rushing mighty wind, and it filled all the house where they were sitting.*
> **Acts 2:1–2**

We know what happens in this great story. They were all filled with the Holy Ghost and began to speak with other tongues as the Spirit gave them utterance. But they were all together, in unity, in worship, waiting.

This is also what we do in a worship time of soaking. We come together in unity, with the same mind, wanting to seek God, hungry to be in His presence. Yes, He is with us always; yes, He never leaves us or forsakes us. But just as the mighty wind entered the room, God's

What Is Soaking?

presence still does physically manifest. There are many times when a group of us are together in worship, not looking at the time but just enjoying Jesus, when we physically sense the weighty love of God come down and rest on us like a blanket. Prophesies and prophetic songs will flow like a river, and healings will take place during worship.

Soaking Is a Great Way to Begin

You can soak in His presence alone at home. There is no rule. Think of it even as a time when you are fellowshipping with Him. You are basking in His sweet love. You are listening to Him. You are putting your mind on Him and only Him.

I do believe that soaking is only the beginning. When we first begin to do this, we are being still and focusing on receiving His love. But as you grow in this, you become stronger and more secure in His love so that you are able to reach back to your heavenly Father, to Jesus, and to the Holy Spirit and give Him of the love that He has given you. That becomes more balanced and more of a true fellowship and communion. The sequence then becomes that you are getting so strong in that oneness that it begins to overflow onto others naturally. You won't be able to help it, for you will be so full of God.

People will begin to see it on your face; you won't be able to hide it! Believe me when I say this. You will shine with God's glory. Joy and laughter and the life of Jesus will be more regular in your life. Let's face it. A person full of the love of God is full of life, real life. They reach out and are not self-centered. They think about others more than themselves, and they are more aware of others' needs and wants. This is the right sequence and what God would have surely. Picture Jesus on the earth. He was so one with God and knew that His Father loved him so. He was truly secure in that love. Jesus was full of joy and peace.

We have a soaking room at our church, Heart Beat International in Colorado Springs, where I bring all my keyboard and guitar and sound equipment twice a month on Sunday nights, and another friend brings his electric guitar and plays. We do a two-hour stretch or longer. There are couches and bean bag chairs all around the room. We dim the lights and put on the candles and totally devote that time to worship. We do things a little different. For the most part, a soaking room will play or sing worship. And all others will be quietly communing with God and soaking in His presence. But ours has become more of that and also of body ministry. The gifts of the Spirit as recorded in 1 Corinthians 14 are present. We give ourselves to God and ask Him to use us however He wants. We sing to him all together in tongues or English, and we worship Him. Much of the time I am singing and leading in prophetic worship and singing the Word of God. Every evening is different. Sometimes there are needs, and we will gather around and pray for that person. But we all leave full and ministered to and so encouraged by His love. So our soaking is more interactive; maybe we are not a true soaking room, but we are still blessed. Both are good; both have a purpose. One is to minister to God and to each other. The other type of soaking is to be still and listen to God speak to you and to bask in His ever present love.

Most people, even Christians, are not fully aware of how much they are loved by God. And hence, that is why we need to learn to soak —to take His love in and the thought of how He is passionate about us. Knowing God's love doesn't just hit you. It could happen by a miracle, yes. But most of the time, you will need to take the Scriptures and meditate on them regarding God's love. You must grow into that knowledge as well as by soaking. I once was pondering the thought of how people on this imperfect earth don't understand about God's love. And here we have an enemy that tries to distract us from finding out about it. With the trials and imperfections of this

What Is Soaking?

life, surely we don't just need a drink of His love once in a while. But we need huge daily doses while on this earth. Jesus said, *"Sufficient unto the day is the evil thereof"* (Matthew 6:34). So if we face daily evil, then we need daily bread and daily love rations. The wonderful thing is that we can have as much of His love as we want. There are no measly portions here!

Be Still

> *Be **still** and **know** that I am God: I will be exalted among the heathen, I will be exalted in the earth.*
> **Psalm 46:10**

Still-7503 Rahpah: This Hebrew word speaks of relaxing, dropping down, to sink or fall. To throw and to cast down.

Know-3045 Yada: This Hebrew word speaks of perceiving or acquiring knowledge. Becoming acquainted with.

God-430 Elohim: This is the Hebrew word for God that is plural. Gods. So it is speaking truly of the trinity here.

To be still is to be still. To stop everything else and think about God. To realize that He is great and we are not. I had this experience very powerfully when I took a trip with my family to see the Grand Canyon in Arizona. When I first saw it, I was still, so taken back by the greatness of God. I truly sensed His presence and was in awe of Him. I just stood there and stared. I didn't have the words to say. That this magnificent Creator could make such a thing, never mind how it all happened. The truth is God did it to show His mighty power and His glory.

The more we stop and be still, the more we will experience Him. He wants us to. He's not hiding. A good father loves to have his children around him. He wants us to know how good He is and how tenderly He loves us.

I do believe that as we learn to do this as a way of life, only more of the supernatural will follow. Dreams, visions, and visitations are for those who are hungry and are willing to pursue Him. Pursue His presence. Get lost in Him, and let Him take you places. Let Him love you deeply and heal your heart. Sing to Him; He loves when we sing from our hearts. He's waiting for you to come.

In reading the book, *The Power to Change the World,* by Rick Joyner, we can learn the history of two great revivals in the early 1900s. In the years long ago of 1904–1906 were the greatest revivals of our time in Wales and in Azusa, California. If first began in Wales with hungry hearts that spent time with Him and were faithful to pray and wait and to seek His face. It paid off. Evan Roberts was the evangelist greatly used in the revival in Wales, which spread like wildfire throughout many cities and towns with over 70,000 converts. News spread to America, and there were a few hungry hearts that were crying out for revival to come to them. Frank Bartleman and William Seymour were two of the main vessels God mightily used in Los Angeles. Bartleman wrote a letter to Evan Roberts in Wales and asked him to pray for them in California. Evan said he would, and he gave this advice: "Congregate the people together who are willing to make a total surrender. Pray and wait. Believe God's promises. Hold daily meetings." Azusa turned out to be an even greater revival.

There are so many books written about these two revivals; you must study for yourself to find all the wonderful details. But it comes down to hunger and time. The time spent will depend on how hungry you are. What you sow you will reap. And God knows the heart and how serious we are. No one can play games with God, for He sees all.

Chapter Seven – We Need His Refreshing

When I was in my early forties and married with two young preteen kids, I had an open vision one night. I was getting ready for bed on a typical, ordinary weeknight. I turned out the light and climbed into bed. Our bedroom had high ceilings, and on the outside upper wall, a triangle of glass inset, which faced the backyard in which there were no trees. An open vision on the opposite wall appeared, way up at the top of the wall. There were trees waving in the wind; they were on fire but yet stayed green and alive. This vision stayed a few minutes. I thought I was seeing things and kept blinking and even looked outside the window but realized we didn't have any trees out back, and it was not windy outside.

For the longest time, I tried to figure out what the Lord was saying. I was a worship leader at the time, and although we had really cool music, there was no fire in our hearts. There was something that we needed. We did worship in the service. But honestly, I can speak for myself. I didn't worship Him at home so much in my private time. In fact, it is sad to tell you that at that time, I felt like I was in a desert. But I was not spiritually mature to understand and put my finger on the why of it. I just knew something was missing. And best I could tell about what God was saying to me that night was this: We are the trees, and He wants us to be verdantly green, rich, and flourishing but yet at the same time continually on fire for Him.

I was saved, and I was not in sin. I was starving for something I didn't know I needed. It was Him. I needed to run to Jesus and receive of His nurturing love. I needed to submerge myself in His holy presence and drench my weary heart. It wasn't a self-help how to book that I needed. I needed living waters and the source of all life. Living on this imperfect earth, we encounter trials and unhappy people even in our everyday encounters with strangers doing errands. There are bills to be paid, meals to be cooked, and clothes to be washed. The errands never end; you buy groceries, and then you have to buy them again. Even the small things that we face daily…how do we think we can keep this all up without a place to run to for refreshment? Some run to the wrongs things. But we were made to run to the God of our new Covenant, the one whose well never runs dry. He meant for us to run to Him, not once in a while, not just on Sunday, or Wednesday, or a once a year retreat. No! It is to be continuous, especially while we live on this imperfect earth where there is an enemy wanting to devour us and our families. I could not keep going on in the way I was going and expect to be totally strong and vibrant to tackle each new day. On our own strength, we will always be failures. We need His strength, we need His love, and we need His presence. And He is more than willing to give us all that we want and need whenever we come to Him. I needed to change my thinking.

Acts 3:19 *Repent…*

God is Looking for Heart Worshipers

*Amplified - So repent (change your mind and purpose); turn around and return [to God] that your sins may be erased (blotted out, wiped clean), that times of **refreshing** (of recovering from the effects of heat, of reviving with fresh air) may come from the presence of the Lord.*

*Voice - So now you need to rethink everything and turn to God, so your sins will be forgiven and a new day can dawn, days of **refreshing** times flowing from the Lord.*

This is the only verse in the New Testament that mentions the word "refreshing." It is telling us that it is God's presence that brings the refreshing. And it is also telling those that do not know Him to turn around and repent. Come and receive forgiveness of sins. Come and become the children of God so that you, too, can enjoy His refreshing presence. We are living on an imperfect earth in which there is an enemy roaming around seeking whom he may devour. And although the battle has been won by our Savior and Champion Jesus Christ, the enemy still seeks to devour and bring us down by lying to us, planting seeds of anything he can to pull us down and bring destruction. But we can go from glory to glory by His Word and by basking in regular times of refreshing in the Lord's presence. We only need to come. There are times that even His children need to be corrected and to change their thinking to repent and draw near to God.

Times of Refreshing

In the U.S. in particular cities like Seattle and Oregon, it rains very often and thus produces lush growth and beautiful, green gardens.

Their weather is known for it in those parts of the U.S.

Compare this to the spiritual realm. What if we could be that way?

Lush and green, always flourishing. We can. But it requires times in His peaceful presence, waiting on Him, worshipping Him, receiving from His generous heart, and fellowshipping with Him.

The word *refreshing* in the Greek is anapsysis.

"A Cooling Refreshing." In the Vines Dictionary, it is "Obtaining Relief."

I believe this to mean that the spiritual atmosphere is changed when the manifestation of the Holy Spirit arrives. Let's read now this verse in the King James Version:

> *Repent ye therefore, and be converted, that your sins may be blotted out, when the times of refreshing shall come from the **presence** of the Lord.*
>
> **Acts 3:19**

The word "presence" in the Greek is *"prosopon."* There are 55 times that this Greek word is used as "Face." It means "the face, the front of the human head, countenance, look."

You see, even though we may not see Him, living in His presence should be normal for us. When we come into worship, His presence is there, and we will be refreshed. But if we sin, we are the ones that have created the wall, the wall of guilt and condemnation, which will keep us away from Him. Sin will cause us to hide like Adam and Eve. And those that don't know Him, their spirit is a sin nature. They may be in an atmosphere where there is worship and the strong presence of God is there. They will sense His peace. All they have to do is receive of Jesus, believe in Jesus, and be changed. They can be forgiven and washed white as snow in an instant and then enjoy His presence daily. God is holy, and we must walk holy. We must reverence His presence and not take it lightly. If we began to walk in strife, jealousy, and unforgiveness—all of this is sin—

slowly we would drift away from spending time with Him, most likely because of the guilt. But really, we were meant to walk in love and enjoy continuously His fellowship and friendship. It strengthens us to keep going. God's presence brings freedom. The bottom line is "Turn around and receive of His forgiveness so that you can enjoy Him." A good example is in **Acts 4:31**, when the Apostles came together:

And when they had prayed, the place was shaken where they were assembled together; and they were all filled with the Holy Ghost, and they spake the word of God with boldness.

He strengthened them and imparted to them as they came in unity with prayer.

In the light of the kings countenance is life; and his favor is as a cloud of the latter rain.

Proverbs 16:15

This word "countenance" in the Old Testament is also speaking of His face, His presence, surrounding you, enveloping you.

For where two or three are gathered together in my name, there am I in the midst of them.

Matthew 18:20

Let's look at the word "refresh" in the online Merriam Webster dictionary.

Refresh—To restore strength and animation, to revive. To freshen up. To renovate, restore, or maintain by renewing supply.

It makes me think of when we have had a good rain. In fact, as I am writing this, it has been raining all day long. We are in the beginning of October here in Colorado Springs, and the fall is here;

Linda Patarello

the leaves are changing and blowing in the wind. But after a good soak, the air is clean and clear; it smells wonderfully fresh. I want to look at some other physical examples just to get you thinking and your imagination going:

-A new mom is exhausted from staying up nights with no sleep, feeding her baby every two hours. The thought of a nice hot shower is so refreshing.

-A homeless person who has slept on the concrete for months is given the blessing of a night in a hotel room with new toiletries, clean clothes, and new shoes. He feels like a new man. He is refreshed.

-A soldier who is in battle night after night, exhausted, filthy, sweaty, and hungry, finally gets relieved to come back to the base and get a hot meal and a good night's rest.

These are only physical examples, and you can imagine many more on your own. But what is it like to be spiritually refreshed?

You have allowed the thoughts on fear or worry to stay and take hold.

You haven't been to church in a while and haven't read your Bible or spent any time in worship. You lose the right perspective. You believe the lies of the enemy. You smell of trials and mental battles. Someone invites you to church, and the worship is flowing. The aroma of heaven is permeating the atmosphere. You begin to remember who you are. You are light, not darkness. The light of His presence begins to break through the crust of black that is trying to encircle your mind and emotions. A holy and loving refreshment comes and washes over you.

This is true refreshing. But how much better would it be if you just stayed in fellowship with Him and kept out the darkness? If you put your foot down and did not allow any fear to trespass into your mind? What if you stood your ground and only let the light come in each day? Then when you are in worship, growth upon growth would come. A deeper walk would increase. You would go from glory to glory, staying refreshed. This is the way I believe it is meant to be.

Now when they saw the boldness of Peter and John, and perceived that they were unlearned and ignorant men, they marveled; and they took knowledge of them, that they had been with Jesus.

Acts 4:13

Chapter Eight – Living Can Be Worship

Over the last few years, I have begun to keep a dream journal. I enjoy discovering what they may mean spiritually. God speaks to us in our dreams. I have found that snow represents the glory of God in dreams. One day I was up in Woodland Park, Colorado, in a warm cabin looking through the window, peering out at the forest as the snow was falling and covering the ground as a blanket as it also fell on the branches of the tall forest trees. I began to ponder on how snow falls and how it is a parallel of how the glory also falls and covers us. The natural aspect is that snow falls on the branches of the trees. But the stronger the tree is, the more it is capable of carrying the snow on its branches. The tiny, young, immature trees could not handle much snow. It takes time for the trees to mature and age, to grow strong and tall. And so it is with us. We represent trees. There are many scriptures that speak on people as trees. Our roots are to grow strong and be established in the love of God. We cannot expect to carry mighty amounts of His glory if we are a young Christian. It takes time to mature and grow in experience with His Word and knowing His ways. Little by little we can handle more glory and more of His power as we grow closer to God the Father and the Son and discover the flow of the Holy Spirit.

On that same day, I asked the Holy Spirit, "How can I grow and discover more of you? How can I stretch myself further in you?

Can you give me some exercise in doing so?" I believe I heard Him say, "See me. Sense me in whatever room you are in. Believe I am there as my Word says." What I understood is that I can use my imagination and picture His power covering every inch of air space. I thought about it more and more. **Psalm 139** says that He is everywhere. So regardless of what I felt, I did this exercise and sensed Him inside of me and all around me. So no matter what I was doing or where I was at, He was with me, and He was there too, listening, watching, keeping me, and loving me. And whatever I did, I found that I could worship Him in it. Whether it was washing dishes, changing sheets, driving up the mountain, or waiting in a line at the bank. My life could worship Him. My thoughts could worship Him. It would not make sense to be singing to Him and be thinking thoughts of complaining or criticism at the same time. I am a spirit, soul, and body. And I can worship Him with all my spirit, soul, and body if I choose to. I am free to do so. If I am free to complain, well, in the same way, I am free to praise and be thankful in my thoughts. The more you are keeping a habit of cultivating a thankful attitude, the more you will make your life a whole lot easier. We have the power to make our lives easier or harder by what thoughts we are keeping our minds on. And so your body will really follow suit. It will lean toward sickness or peace in your heart and peace in your body, which will mean more health. **Proverbs 4:23** speaks of how the word of God is life and health to all of your flesh. My thoughts can praise Him. My actions can also praise Him by putting on kindness and gentleness, humility and patience. These are the fruit of the Spirit, but they show themselves in our actions when we make a decision to move in them. The more you move in these actions, the more you will be developed in them, the same way you develop muscles. You use them and work them, and eventually other people will see your muscles. Yes, in the same way, other people will see your gentleness.

Brother Lawrence

We read about Brother Lawrence, a Carmelite monk in the early 1600s. You can find out about his life in the famous book, which is a small book, called *The Practice of the Presence of God*. He was born Nicholas Herman in the Lorraine region of France in 1611. At age eighteen, he experienced a profound conversion. He entered the monastery and worked in the kitchen for fifteen years. He walked in love towards all and was pure in heart to God. He believed that no matter what you did, you could accomplish simple tasks and still be in God's presence, enjoying Him. *"He had no other care at first but faithfully to reject every other thought, that he might perform all his actions for the love of God."* Here are some excerpts from that little books, quotes that are stated from his own letters:

First Letter

"I worshiped Him the oftenest that I could, keeping my mind in His holy presence, and recalling it as often as I found it wandered from Him. I found no small pain in this exercise, and yet I continued it, notwithstanding all the difficulties that occurred, without troubling or disquieting myself when my mind had wandered involuntarily. I made this my business as much all the day long as at the appointed times of prayer; for at all times, every hour, every minute, even in the height of my business, I drove away from my mind everything that was capable of interrupting my thought of God."

Fifth Letter

"I know that for the right practice of it the heart must be empty of all other things, because God will possess the heart alone; and as He cannot possess it alone without emptying it of all besides, so neither can He act there, and do in it what He pleases, unless it be left vacant to Him. There is not in the world a kind of life more sweet and delightful than that of a continual conversation with God. Those only can comprehend it who practice and experience it; yet I do not advise you to do it from that motive. It is not pleasure which we ought to seek in this exercise; but let us do it from a principle of love, and because God would have us."

Further in the book, we find writings about the character of Brother Lawrence. He once said:

"For me the time of action does not differ from the time of prayer, and in the noise and clatter of my kitchen, while several persons are together calling for as many different things, I possess God in as great tranquility as when upon my knees as the Blessed Sacrament."

"We can do little things for God; I turn the cake that is frying on the pan for the love of Him, and that done, if there is nothing else to call me, I prostrate myself in worship before Him, who has given me grace to work; afterwards I rise happier than a king. It is enough for me to pick up but a straw from the ground for the love of God."

God is Looking for Heart Worshipers

Brother Lawrence was not perfect. The book also describes a few years of trials in which he believed he was lost. But he always, only loved God with all of his life. He renounced all desire other than that of living every moment of his life and doing every action for the love of God, giving to Him, in his own words, "The *ALL* for the *ALL*."

He died on Monday, the 12th of February, 1691, at nine o'clock in the morning, without any pain or struggle, without losing in the slightest the use of any of his faculties; Brother Lawrence passed away in the embrace of his Lord and rendered his soul to God in the peace and calm of one who had fallen asleep. Some of his last words were "It is our one business, my brethren, to worship Him and love Him, without thought of anything else." He died as he had lived, practicing the presence of God.

We Were Made to Grow

Practice makes perfect is the saying we've always heard. You don't hit yourself over the head if you miss it and make a mistake. You just keep practicing. We practice other things like individual sports or practicing to be better at an instrument. We practice cooking and learning new languages. We can practice as well living in the presence of God. In whatever we do in this life, we can worship Him with it and, in the midst of it, giving glory to God. If He gave you the talent to fly a plane, then do it for His glory the best that you can. If He gave you the desire to be a mountain climber and the ease of doing it, glorify your Father with this skill. If you have the skill and the gift of welcoming people into your home and whipping up a luscious meal and elegant table for them with the gift of hospitality, then you can glorify God with this gift. He made us each so unique;

there is no one like you, and every single person has been given gifts and talents. As you draw closer to the Lord, growing into a strong tree by His Word, you will uncover and discover these gifts. You won't have to struggle and strive to find it. He will show it to you. He has put desires inside of us.

I am a musician, a singer and songwriter. Why, I can remember when I was five years old a memory that is very clear. We were on the eve of moving the next day. The kids on the block were outside playing, and this was back in the day when it was pretty safe to play outside even at night. It must have been a summer night, and we had a pickup truck parked out front that held some chicken wire cages in the back of the truck. My dad had some new idea that we were moving out of the city to the country, and he wanted to raise rabbits. That lasted about a year. But I applaud his courage to try something entirely new and out of the realm of anything he had ever tried. Anyways, the back flap was down, and I climbed up in the back and made myself a little seat and began to pretend to play the piano on the wired cage. Where did that come from? I believe that God put that inside my heart and wired me that way. Some of these gifts can be sought in our very own characters and personalities. As we learn to live our lives through Jesus, this is when we will blossom.

> *I am the true vine, and my Father is the husbandman. Every branch in me that beareth not fruit he taketh away: and every branch that beareth fruit, he purgeth it, that it may bring forth more fruit. Now ye are clean through the word which I have spoken unto you. Abide in me, and I in you. As the branch cannot bear fruit of itself, except it abide in the vine; no more can ye, except ye abide in me. I am the vine, ye are the branches: He that abideth in me and I in him, the same bringeth forth much fruit: for without me ye can do nothing. If a man abide not in me, he is cast forth as a branch, and is withered; and men gather them, and cast them into the fire,*

God is Looking for Heart Worshipers

and they are burned. If ye abide in me and my words abide in you, ye shall ask what ye will, and it shall be done unto you. Herein is my Father glorified, that ye bear much fruit; so shall ye be my disciples. As the Father hath loved me, so have I loved you: continue ye in my love. If ye keep my commandments, ye shall abide in my love; even as I have kept my Father's commandments, and abide in his love...

John 15:1–10

As you read further, I believe that abiding in Jesus is to abide in His love. But first you must meditate on the Scriptures and realize His love for you. As you do this, it will begin to overflow naturally onto others. You won't be able to help it. But you can't love others well until you realize the priceless value that Jesus places on your life. He gave all that He had for you. You are His pearl of great price. You must see this, and not just in your simple head. You must realize it deep in your heart. That is revelation knowledge. For then you can love others deeply, as God loves Jesus and as Jesus loves you, and you will love others and lay your life down for them.

This is when fruit is produced—ripe, sweet, luscious fruit. Remember, a tree does not strive and strain to produce fruit. It is a natural sequence of events. The fruit is born from the branch, and the branch is sucking the juice and life from the trunk and the root system. And roots are established in the rich soil. So let your life worship God, and let your light SHINE!

Chapter Nine – Using Your Imagination

Every person was born with an imagination, and even when we are very small, we begin to pretend and use our imagination. We pretend we are doctors, and the toy store even makes a toy doctor bag with all the goodies in it so that we can test it out on our pretend patients. We play with dolls and have fun with dress up costumes. There are even children's museums that have special sections where kids can dress up and pretend.

Imagination in and of itself is not bad, just as the dollar bill is not bad; it is a tool. And we can use it for good or for evil. I believe the imagination was a God-given gift to us for we are made in His image. God has an imagination. He uses it to create with. And we do the same. Everything begins with a picture thought in our imagination. When we are going to do something, we first picture it. Think about it. When you want to bake a cake, you first think, *What kind? Ah, maybe chocolate with chocolate frosting.* When you plan a trip of errands for the day, you picture the street routes you are going to take. When a person builds a house, they first have to have a picture, and then the planning can start. We think in pictures; this is how we are wired.

The enemy knows this, and that is why he uses the media and the billboards in advertising to create pictures for anything that will sell and get our attention. Some things may be harmless. Sometimes it's junk food, and sometimes it is evil like pornography or liquor. Have you noticed that the TV shows are getting more and more evil? He knows that a picture can steer a person into sin. A picture is nothing that should be taken lightly. It is the beginning of a seed that is planted in our mind, then into the heart it goes and grows. Watching movies of violence or horror is like playing with dynamite. You may think it's entertainment. But those pictures will come to you, before your eyes. Romans 8:6 speaks of being carnally minded, that it is death—a slow death for sure. The same is also true if we go in the opposite direction and use it for good.

I believe that the imagination is the link between the physical and the spiritual realm. It's like a bridge that leads from the city to the country. You go back and forth to get from one place to the other. You drive on it and use it to get to where you want to go. Let's first look at the very first place in the Old Testament where we can find the word "imagination."

> *...keep this forever in the **imagination** of the thoughts of the heart of thy people, and prepare their heart unto thee.*
>
> **1 Chronicles 29:18**
>
> *God saw that the wickedness of man was great in the earth, and that every **imagination** of the thoughts of his heart was only evil continually.*

God is Looking for Heart Worshipers

Genesis 6:5

The Hebrew Word for this word is: Yeser (#3336 Strong's Concordance) meaning: Form, frame, make, conception, thing, framed.

So it is a framework we are building when we imagine, whether it's good or bad. The next scripture has this same Hebrew word, but it is translated as "mind."

> *Thou wilt keep him in perfect peace, whose **mind** (Yeser) is stayed on thee.*

Isaiah 26:3

So as you imagine and keep your mind on God, even picturing Him on His glorious throne, beholding Him in His beauty, and thinking of His wonderful mercies, He will keep you in perfect peace. Your imaginations will create thoughts, and as you dwell on those good thoughts, these seeds will be planted in your heart and will begin to grow and bring life.

Let's look again at the scripture in **1 Chronicles 29**. If you look closely, you can see a pattern or a sequence of steps happening. First comes the imagination, which is the pictures in your mind, then the thoughts are built from those pictures. This then causes those thoughts to drop down into your heart, which brings growth to bring evil or growth to bring good things in your life.

> *...keep this forever in the **imagination** of the **thoughts** of the **heart** of thy people, and prepare their heart unto thee.*

1 Chronicles 28:18

> *God saw that the wickedness of man was great in the earth, and that every imagination of the thoughts of his heart was only evil continually.*

Linda Patarello

Genesis 6:5

So you see, the imagination is a gift from God that should be used wisely to bring about good things. But man has a free will to choose which way he will use it. People can choose to use it for evil, thinking on drugs or violence, which will end up bringing it to pass. And then they blame God for the circumstance that they end up in, when in reality it was their own imagination that created the evil thoughts, which grew and entered their heart, and that caused the action to happen. They brought the end result of circumstances on themselves. God often gets the blame.

Examples of Imagination in Worship

Well now, how can we use our imagination in worship? It can carry us into the presence of God for sure. I have experienced this over and over, and it only draws you closer to the Lord and causes your relationship with Him to grow stronger and closer. In the last chapter, I shared how Brother Lawrence practiced the presence of God. He put his mind on the fact that God was all around him whether night or day, and so he worshiped God in everything he did. But the key is he practiced it. So must we practice to worship God using our imaginations. This is not just a Sunday thing at church that you do. How close do you want to draw to God? You can have as much of Jesus as you want. But it won't happen automatically. You must give of yourself to Him. Clear your mind, and put His thoughts in there. I begin by finding a quiet place in my house. The more time you have to do this, the better and faster you will grow in it. We can use our time for good.

I usually have the Bible next to me, and I might begin by meditating on a scripture and picturing it. There are so many wonderful scriptures that are great pictures we can use in worship. For instance:

God is Looking for Heart Worshipers

Then the angel showed me the river of the water of life, as clear as crystal, flowing from the throne of God and of the Lamb down the middle of the great street of the city. On each side of the river stood the tree of life, bearing twelve crops of fruit, yielding its fruit every month. And the leaves of the tree are for the healing of the nations. No longer will there be any curse. The throne of God and of the Lamb will be in the city, and his servants will serve him. They will see his face, and his name will be on their foreheads. There will be no more night. They will not need the light of a lamp or the light of the sun, for the Lord God will give them light. And they will reign for ever and ever.

Revelation 22:1–5

You can meditate on this picture. The more you do, the more your imagination will create it. It will become so clear that you will feel like you're there. You can close your eyes and worship God doing this. Many times I will put on some soft worship music, soaking worship music. This will help relax you and put the distractions aside. But if you don't have that, it's okay; it can still work. You can train your mind to stay fixed on God. Many times I go to sleep doing this, and the Holy Spirit will begin to speak to me.

What you are doing is activating your imagination. As you begin and stay there, the Lord will step in and minister to you. He may show you further things or places. But you must test it and line it up with Scripture. Sometimes there will not be a scripture for what He shows you. Then you must lean on the truths of the Bible. Does it edify and bring peace and freedom? Is it based on the love of God? Because God is love and will never tell you to do something destructive. He is truth and not deception or condemnation.

This is very powerful and a great tool to be used in worship. There are times when in worship I will picture myself walking down the shore with Jesus, watching the sunset. Or I am on the back of His horse as He is riding us on the cliffs overlooking the sea; I will feel the wind running through my hair.

I receive of God's love during these times. If the Bible says that God is love, and in John 3:16 it says that God SO LOVED the world, I will picture the Father telling me that He dearly loves me and thinks only good and precious thoughts of me. I will listen and hear the voice of Jesus saying, "I love you so much. I don't regret at all the pain I went through for you. I gave my all for you."

I can't see the Holy Spirit, but I will still imagine what He looks like. He speaks to us all the time. You can picture heaven. Picture yourself in the very throne room on your face before God the Father. These can be very powerful worship times. I often will be overcome by the love of God and the very presence of God, and all I can do is weep and worship.

When we don't know Him or His great love, we cannot truly love ourselves. So it is hard to picture the Father God looking at us and telling us how much He loves us. Our head just goes tilt. Forget about all the past. To change, we must receive of His love. If you don't, you won't see change. I really believe this. It is His love that changes you. You can't help but be changed when you are in His presence, hearing Him say good things to you and about you. You just melt like chocolate. We so desperately need this! Make yourself push past what you think, what you did, and the mistakes you made. Close that door.

An Exercise

Get alone by yourself where you can close your eyes and get still. Imagine Jesus entering the room and standing in front of you. His eyes are only on one place, and that's you. But see a smile on His face. His eyes are so full of tenderness toward you. He is glowing because He is light and full of love and glory. There is no darkness in Him. He is strong. Then you hear Him speak your name. He

God is Looking for Heart Worshipers

actually says your name. He knows you, everything about you, before you were even born. Now hear Him say, "I love you so much. You are the reason I came to this earth. I forgive you. When I think of you, I smile. You put a smile on my face."

You see, all of these things can be backed up by the Word of God. So why would it be wrong to imagine them happening to you? After I have had some time in His presence, worshiping and praising Him, thanking Him and receiving love from Him, and I get up and walk away, I feel so refreshed, so completely peaceful. There is nothing like it. You begin to love yourself because God loves you. If He loves and forgives you, then you can love and forgive you.

Chapter Ten – Worship Has an Aroma

I remember sitting up in my room one summer night with the window open wide. I was looking up into the night sky and listening to singing. This was in my college years when I was still new in the Word of God, and getting to know Jesus more. On this particular night, what I heard was a sound of a group singing worship songs. We had apartments in back of us and an alley that separated the apartments from our house. They may have been having a Bible study. But this was my first experience with the Lord opening my spiritual senses to the supernatural sense of smell. If we have spiritual eyes to see, and the Bible calls us a spirit man, well, we must have a spiritual nose to go with our spiritual eyes. Anyways, as I was sitting near the window listening to the beautiful, soothing sounds of voices singing praises to God, I began to smell roses. The fragrance of roses wafted through the air into my window. Of course, I began to cry to think that Jesus knew where I was and that He would minister to me this way. It made me cry even more because in our backyard at the time, there were no roses or any flowers there. All the flowers were in the front yard. God sees us when no one else does. He can do anything. I believe He let me smell the fragrance of their worship to Him. And the sounds of their voices were ministering to me. If they only knew.

When I first began to realize that worship had a fragrance, I was reading the story in **John 12** about Mary, who was anointing the feet of Jesus. Let's take a look at that scripture.

> *Then Jesus six days before the passover came to Bethany, where Lazarus was, which had been dead, whom he raised from the dead. There they made him a supper; and Martha served: but Lazarus was one of them that sat at the table with him. Then took Mary a pound of ointment of spikenard, very costly, and anointed the feet of Jesus, and wiped his feet with her hair: and the house was filled with the odour of the ointment.*
>
> **John 12:1–3**

There is so much wisdom and revelation treasures here to understand. In those days, it was a hospitality act to wash the feet of your guests. This was performed generally by a servant of a Jewish household because of the idea of defilement in connection with the feet and with the dirt. The servants would unlatch the sandals. Shoes were not worn in the house but left outside because shoes touched the dirty ground.

Mary put herself into a servant position. Also, **1 Corinthians 11:15** speaks of a woman's long hair being given to her as a covering; it is a glory to her. This was actually a prophetic act whether she was aware of it or not. Even Jesus confirmed that. He said in verse 7, "Against the day of my burying hath she kept this." She was anointing His feet with her glory in order to prepare them to take the nails for our sakes.

The same accounts in Mark and in Matthew are different in that they speak that she anointed His head. However, we will look at the account in John. It would make more sense for her to be wiping His feet with her hair than his head. Either way, she was preparing him for burial.

When a person truly worships God, they are only focused on one thing: Him. Not themselves, not their appearance, not what people may think of them. They don't care about anything but the one they are worshiping. This was Mary. It was true worship from the heart. The other thing I see is that worship does something. Worship acts. It all stems from the heart. But out of the heart comes an action. You can't help it. You have to do something for it is coming from your heart. It is overflowing out of your heart. My grandbaby, when he was almost two years old, was walking around in his living room, and we had the music playing for children. This one song had such a great beat. He had something in his hand, and you could see this look on his face of serious purpose. He walked over to the coffee table and put his toy down. And then he began to dance with such a rhythm and a purpose. He couldn't help it. It was coming from the inside of him. True worship will cause to do something, whether it's putting your hands up, laying face down on the ground, kneeling, shouting, or singing at the top of your lungs. It will bring an action. The person in the back with no lips moving, no motion, and no smile makes me wonder what is going on in their head. Are they worried about what others are thinking of them? I don't know. All I know is, to love takes action, and to worship takes action. I believe all of the times on earth that we worshiped from our hearts, God will remember, and I believe you will be rewarded.

In the physical realm, as she poured that ointment onto His feet, the scripture said that the odor **filled** the room. The word filled in the

Greek is pleroo, to be complete. Since she was worshiping from her heart, I believe this is a parallel to the spiritual realm. True worship from our hearts also causes an aroma to fill the room in the spirit, which also reaches to God. He smells our worship. He knows if it is fake or real. Real worship gives off a fragrance. But don't take my word for it. There are more scriptures to prove this.

There were tons of animals sacrificed to God in the Old Testament. The people may have smelled a wonderful barbecue smell, but many scriptures state, "it was a sweet savor to God."

Noah, after the flood, offered a sacrifice to God in **Genesis 8:21**. It says it was a sweet savor to God. You will find many scriptures of "a sweet savor unto the Lord" in Exodus, Leviticus, and Numbers.

A sweet, savory smell always speaks of obedience and a right heart, whereas a bad smell would mean a rebelliousness to the Lord.

Rebellion

> *Hear, O earth: behold, I will bring evil upon this people, even the fruit of their thoughts, because they have not hearkened unto my words, nor to my law, but rejected it.*
>
> *To what purpose cometh there to me incense from Sheba, and the sweet cane from a far country?* ***your burnt offerings are not acceptable, nor your sacrifices sweet unto me.***
>
> **Jeremiah 6:19–20**

Obedience

> *For in mine holy mountain, in the mountain of the height of Israel, saith the Lord GOD, there shall all the house of Israel, all of them in the land, serve me: there will I accept them, and there will I require your offerings, and the firstfruits of your oblations, with all your holy things.* ***I will accept you with***

your sweet savour, when I bring you out from the people, and gather you out of the countries wherein ye have been scattered; and I will be sanctified in you before the heathen.

Ezekiel 20:40–41

Now we read in the New Testament about sweet-smelling fragrances.

Now thanks be unto God, which always causeth us to triumph in Christ, and maketh manifest the savour of his knowledge by us in every place.

*For we are unto God **a sweet savour of Christ**, in them that are saved, and in them that perish: To the one we are the **savour of death** unto death; and to the other the **savour of life** unto life.*

2 Corinthians 2:14–16

The word "savour" in the Greek here speaks of "euodia"—a sweet smelling fragrance; incense; an odor of satisfaction, pleasing to God.

*And walk in love, as Christ also hath loved us, and hath given himself for us an offering and a sacrifice to God for **a sweet-smelling savour.***

Ephesians 5:2

But I have all, and abound: I am full, having received of Epaphroditus the things which were sent from you, an odour of a sweet smell, a sacrifice acceptable, well-pleasing to God.

Philippians 4:18

If you read through Song of Solomon, you will find many references to perfume. For love is sweet and has a sweet smelling fragrance. **Proverbs 27:9** says that *Ointment and perfume rejoice the heart.*

Why is it that we have all these wonderful women's perfume and men's cologne counters in the shopping malls? We want to smell good. We want to give off a pleasing aroma. Where does this come from? I think it is representative of the spiritual world, in the same way flowers smell sweet and beautiful. But in the opposite way, wilted flowers that are beginning to decompose begin to stink. Rotten vegetables stink. Rebellion stinks.

My wounds stink and are corrupt because of my foolishness.

Psalm 38:5

...I have made the stink of your camps to come up unto your nostrils; yet have ye not returned unto me, saith the LORD.

Amos 4:10

An Aroma from Heaven

I will end this chapter by telling you of another experience in which the Lord allowed me to smell in the supernatural but with my own physical nose.

It was on a Wednesday night at a church I was serving in, in Colorado Springs. We were just about to go up onto the stage and begin worship. I was down and sad for some reason. It was a few minutes before we were about to begin. As I began to walk around to the steps on the side of the stage, this clear aroma was leading me. It was so pungent, I inhaled as far as I could and then kept on taking deep breaths. It was as if something was leading me onto the stage.

An angel? Jesus? I don't know. I didn't see anything, only smelled. And then when the service began, the smell only stayed and got stronger. No one else seemed to be smelling this. They didn't look out of the ordinary. No one said anything. But the smell got stronger to me and ministered to me so deeply. I knew it was God. I knew it was supernatural. It smelled of a combination of things—incense, patchouli oil—it was a deep, spicy aroma. But at the same time it brought back so many memories of my life rolled into one smell. This is really the only way I can describe it. We minister to God with a sweet-smelling aroma. But then He ministers to us with the same.

When you come down to it, it truly is all about love.

Chapter Eleven – The Pure in Heart Shall See God

I used to ask God, "Show me how to come to you, Lord. Show me how to get into your presence." Now there is getting to be all kinds of wonderful teachings and books. You can find some great stuff on the Internet. But before it was not so easy. Even pastors weren't readily teaching on this, because they didn't totally know themselves.

But as you meditate on the Word of God, the Holy Spirit will unravel the mysteries that are there for you to find. Jesus gave us some clues, and I'm so grateful that He did. They are all in the Bible. Sometimes we overlook the verses that are so commonly known and don't realize that the answers can be right under our very nose. God hides them for us, not from us. But it's up to us to seek them out, like searching for buried treasure.

We are going to find some gems in the Beatitudes. You could even title it "Be of These Attitudes." The Beatitudes is actually a sequence of events or levels. You surrender yourself to each step. Jesus is showing us the character or qualities of Himself and those who are living in heaven.

Matthew 5

1. *And seeing the multitudes, he went up into a mountain: and when he was set, his disciples came unto him:*
2. *And he opened his mouth, and taught them, saying,*
3. *Blessed are the poor in spirit: for theirs is the kingdom of heaven.*
4. *Blessed are they that mourn: for they shall be comforted.*
5. *Blessed are the meek: for they shall inherit the earth.*
6. *Blessed are they which do hunger and thirst after righteousness: for they shall be filled.*
7. *Blessed are the merciful: for they shall obtain mercy.*
8. *Blessed are the pure in heart: for they shall see God.*
9. *Blessed are the peacemakers: for they shall be called the children of God.*
10. *Blessed are they which are persecuted for righteousness' sake: for theirs is the kingdom of heaven.*
11. *Blessed are ye, when men shall revile you, and persecute you, and shall say all manner of evil against you falsely, for my sake.*
12. *Rejoice, and be exceeding glad: for great is your reward in heaven: for so persecuted they the prophets which were before you.*

The Beatitudes are levels and a sequence. I believe the closer you get to God, the more you become like Jesus but also the more the world will hate you. But God will show His favor. It is inevitable. Let's read verse 3 out of the Amplified Bible.

Poor in Spirit

Vs. 3: Blessed (happy, to be envied, and spiritually prosperous—with life-joy and satisfaction in God's favor and salvation, regardless of their outward conditions) are the poor in spirit (the humble, who rate themselves insignificant), for theirs is the kingdom of heaven!

So "blessed" is about being happy, to be envied, and having all of God's favor on you. He's saying blessed are the poor in spirit, for theirs is the kingdom of heaven. This is speaking of the poor being the unsaved. They can rejoice because the gift of salvation has come knocking on their door. The kingdom of heaven is being given to them freely so that they don't have to stay poor in spirit any more. Get your eyes off of poor you and onto Jesus, who is your answer.

Those Who Mourn

Vs. 4: Blessed are they that mourn: for they shall be comforted.

Once you are saved and come into the kingdom, becoming one of His own, you may need comfort from all of the past, comfort from pain or all of the time you have been an orphan, away from your heavenly Father. Blessed are you for you shall receive comfort! The comfort that is to heal your heart. For Jesus paid for this comfort. He paid for your grief on the cross. He carried it. To get a person to a state of being secure to go on with growing healthy, you must first be healed and mended. He wants the best for you. God wants you to grow and be mature. You are not meant to stay as a baby Christian.

Even in the natural, babies grow into toddlers, then into children, then teens, and then finally adults. This is life. This is what God also wants in the spirit: healthy, strong sons. We in the kingdom are all referred to as sons once we mature.

The Meek

Vs. 5: Blessed are the meek: for they shall inherit the earth.

The next level is meekness. After you are comforted, you have a choice to humble yourself so that you can learn. To be humble is to be teachable. If you want to go on with God and grow, you must be humble. And this is something we do ourselves. The mentality in heaven, the way of those that live in heaven, is humility. Not every believer humbles themselves. You can go through all of your life without being humbled. But if you want to grow, if you want to be close to God, to Jesus, and to the Holy Spirit, the way is humility. All of these traits, Jesus did. He was meek. So we are to follow His example.

To be meek in the world is to be unseen, shy, and unimportant. You are not popular at all. You may think, if that is so, how will God find me at all? The world says, "I need to make something of myself," or "I am making my way to the top. Everybody better get out of my way." God's way is different. Quite the opposite. The way of heaven is to be a servant. The top is the bottom. And believe me, if you do that, He will see you. In fact, I believe you will be like a magnet to
Him!

This one is SO vital that I want to spend more time on it.

Meek - 4239 Greek is Prays—Gentle, mild, meek. The opposite of self assertion.

God is Looking for Heart Worshipers

When you look up the word in the online dictionary of Merriam Webster and find all the opposite antonyms, this is some of what you find:

arrogant, bumptious, chesty, conceited, egotistic (or egotistical), fatuous, haughty, highfalutin (also hifalutin), high-and-mighty, high-handed, high-hat, hoity-toity, huffish, huffy, imperious, lordly, overweening, peremptory, pompous, presuming, presumptuous, pretentious, self-asserting, self-assertive, supercilious, superior, toplofty (also toploftical), uppish, uppity

A proud person is not meek. A proud person thinks he knows everything, so therefore he is not teachable.

> *Though the LORD be high, yet hath he respect unto the lowly: but the **proud** he knoweth afar off.*
>
> **Psalm 138:6**

God loves the humble. In this day and age, it is not easy to be humble. But we must fight to stay humble. We can do it for this is our new nature in Christ. When you are meek, you are low, humble, quiet, and a servant. You may think sometimes, I don't have a fancy degree or position. You could say, I never finished high school. I don't have a lot of ability. Good. You meet the requirements then.

God uses nobodies. It is one of His specialties. Sometimes our fancy titles can give us a big head. There's nothing wrong with them. But He is our everything, not us.

Staying low is preferred. When you are low, God knows where to find you. He found David as a boy in the fields with the sheep. Jesus is our example. And it is so strange because you don't end up low. He exalts you. But let Him do it and not you.

> *But He giveth more grace. Wherefore he saith, God resisteth the proud, but giveth grace unto the humble.*

Linda Patarello

James 4:6

Humble yourselves therefore under the mighty hand of God, that he may exalt you in due time.

1 Peter 5:6

Warning to Walk Humbly

The more you want to be used by God and His power and His gifts, the more you need to keep yourself humble. Wear humility as a coat. ALWAYS give God the glory. For it belongs to Him and only Him. Everything we have comes from God and not of ourselves.

But God hath chosen the foolish things of the world to confound the wise; and God hath chosen the weak things of the world to confound the things which are mighty;

And base things of the world, and things which are despised, hath God chosen, yea, and things which are not, to bring to nought things that are:

That no flesh should glory in his presence.

But of him are ye in Christ Jesus, who of God is made unto us wisdom, and righteousness, and sanctification, and redemption:

That, according as it is written, He that glorieth, let him glory in the Lord.

1 Corinthians 1:27–31

The Hungry for God

Vs. 6: Blessed are they which do hunger and thirst after righteousness: for they shall be filled.

The next level is learning. But first always comes a teachable heart, which is meekness. The prerequisite is to get pride out of your life and keep it out! Knowledge comes from God and His word, not our own heady thoughts. Keep your head out of the way. Do you know that not all are hungry? But if you want to be filled, you must first be hungry. That part is also up to us. Renewing your mind on His word will create hunger. You keep planting the seed of His word, watering it, and speaking and thinking it. It will grow into a lush garden, and then you are going to receive more seed from that garden and can plant a bigger garden in your heart. It's the Word that changes us. So plant the Word, let it grow, and keep reading and watering. God knows how to fill you and keep you satisfied. We were made for His Word. We were made to think so that we could think on His Word.
We were made to grow.

When I first saw all of these truths in the Beatitudes, I saw my life as it has progressed. I used to be poor in spirit and mourning. I had my own share of a sad past and my own fill of crying. He then taught of humility and hungering for His word. I have seen much growth. But I am still walking this out like everyone else.

The Merciful

Vs 7: Blessed are the merciful: for they shall obtain mercy.

Once we are filled with His word and His righteousness, now we are growing. Some don't ever get filled, because they are never hungry. They may only eat of physical food, yet their spirit man is a skinny rail. They feed the stomach but not the mind and the spirit.

To be merciful is to think of others. This is a person who is becoming mature. When we are babies, it's all about us and our diaper, our bottle. We want to eat, and we want it now! We are self-absorbed and self-centered. We somehow think it's important for everyone to hear our problems. Like they really want to hear it. No, they have their own problems. But we don't want to hear theirs; we want them to hear only ours. That is an attitude of a child.

But a grown up begins to see outside of themselves. You begin to see others and their needs. As you do, compassion rises, and you want to help. This is how Jesus was on the earth in the gospels. As you read through the gospels, people constantly asked and shouted, "Have mercy on us, Son of David." And constantly, everywhere he turned, He had mercy and compassion on people and healed and delivered them. This is a good sign; when you and I show mercy, we can be excited. For that means we are growing and maturing and becoming like Jesus! And then what happens? We give and it is given to us, and so it is that we are blessed. We show mercy, and then mercy comes back and it is shown to us. If you show selfishness, you will find people will be selfish back.

The Pure in Heart

Vs. 8: Blessed are the pure in heart: for they shall see God.

Like a child, we must be pure in heart if we want to see God. God is a holy God. To come into His presence, we must be holy. I'm not saying we are perfect on our own. Jesus is the one that made us holy and blameless. This is how God sees us. But we don't take advantage of this and live in sin. Because He pours His love on us and sees us through His Son's work, we want to please Him. We choose to live a holy life. And if we make a mistake, we receive His forgiveness.

> *Therefore, as the elect of God, holy and beloved, put on tender mercies, kindness, humility, meekness, longsuffering; bearing with one another, and forgiving one another…*
>
> **Colossians 3:12–13 NKJV**

God is Looking for Heart Worshipers

For by one offering He has perfected forever those who are being sanctified.

Hebrews 10:14 NKJV

He sees us perfect as Jesus. We know we are not. Only Jesus is perfect. But we are to see ourselves through the work of Jesus. We are being sanctified by His Word. We must keep ourselves pure. It's not a negative thing like "You mean I can't do that anymore?" The more you become like Jesus and fellowship with His Spirit and His Word, the more you want Him and all the heavenly life that goes with Him. It should become a natural desire, where we love righteousness, holiness, and purity. You get to a place where you don't want to hurt or grieve His Spirit. These are the ones that shall see Him. I believe in these last days that are coming, many will be taken up to heaven before His throne to be in His presence, not because they died and it's their time but because they are so in love with God and are holy and hungry for Him that they will have supernatural encounters with Jesus and with the Father. Our hearts must be right, and we must be single-minded, for He is holy. If you are living in strife, unforgiveness, selfishness, and anger, don't expect that you will come into contact in the spirit with the holy, living God.

See - 3700 in Strong's "Optanomai"- To look at, behold.

This is speaking of "to appear, to allow one's self to be seen." This same word was used in **Matthew 17:3** as "appear": *There **appeared** unto them Moses and Elijah, talking with Him.*

> *Jesus said: "Go quickly and tell His disciples...He is risen from the dead, and indeed He is going before into Galilee; there you will **see** Him."*
> **Matthew 28:7 NKJV**

Yes, there are accounts of where Jesus appeared to people in our days that were not believers or living holy lives, but it may have been a one-time thing, unlike people in the past that saw Him on an ongoing basis because they lived holy lives. They have fellowship with Him, and He calls them friends. I want to be one of those, close to His heart, like John the disciple. He is the one who was take up in the spirit in Revelation. We are supernatural beings, where the supernatural should be natural. This is a prophetic time, and the Lord wants us to reach and believe for these things. Jesus was telling us how to posture ourselves in the Beatitudes so that these wonderful, real experiences could happen.

The Peacemakers

> *Vs. 9, NKJV: Blessed are the peacemakers, for they shall be called the sons of God.*

If you are following these levels and using your faith to walk in each level, you are by now getting more disciplined. It takes faith and self control to walk in mercy and holiness, love and meekness. The New King James Version calls you sons, not children.

Peacemakers - 1518 Strong's "Eirenopoios" to love peace.

Get a picture of these believers and see yourself this way. No more babies. No more woundedness but strong believers following Jesus. They act just like Jesus, showing mercy. They please God their Father. These are the overcomers that the book of Revelation speaks of. They are strong pillars. They are showing Jesus on this earth. They are bringing heaven to earth. This is what we are going to see in the last days, and it is already beginning. This is a people that are not satisfied with playing church any longer. They want the real thing. They are hungry for more of God. They love His Word; it is food for them, it is daily bread, and they cannot exist without it.

They spend time regularly with the Father, Son, and Holy Ghost, fellowshipping, worshiping, and loving Him.

Persecution

> *Vs. 10: Blessed are they which are persecuted for righteousness' sake: for theirs is the kingdom of heaven.*

Why is this outcome stated twice as in the first Beatitude in verse 3? Maybe Jesus wanted to remind us when we get persecuted we need to remember who we are and what we have in Him. When we get persecuted, the first thing that we might experience is "Poor me. Why did this happen to me?" We can feel sorry for ourselves. It doesn't feel good. It hurts. So He is reminding you that you are Blessed.

Yours is the kingdom of heaven.

Many will not be persecuted, because they are lukewarm, living in many ways like the world. Only the ones that have gone through all the different levels will be persecuted. For it is inevitable. It is the next level. It is a sequence of events. It will and it must happen. It means you are doing opposite of the world; you are pleasing God. Satan is not happy with you, and he will make sure you are persecuted. He partly will do this because he wants you to back off of your walk but also because he hates the body of Christ. He hates who God loves.

Persecute - 1377 Strong's "Dioko" a verb. To make to run or flee. Put to flight, and drive away in a hostile manner.

Do you remember Paul? He did this to Christians before he became transformed. He went after Christians brutally and killed them.

Linda Patarello

Persecution and Falsely Accused

Vs. 11–12: Blessed are ye, when men shall revile you, and persecute you, and shall say all manner of evil against you falsely, for my sake. Rejoice, and be exceeding glad: for great is your reward in heaven: for so persecuted they the prophets which were before you.

When you reach this point, you are bold as a lion. For the very reason you are being persecuted means you are stepping out and walking by faith in the boldness of the Spirit. Boldness is what we need in these last days. Boldness has been given to the church. If He has given us the gifts and the fruit of the Spirit, then we know we have boldness as well. We have all that we need. Being persecuted means you are doing it right! It's like the old carnivals where you had the sledge hammer and the thermometer that went up to the top. If you hit it right on and hard enough, it dinged. The persecution is your "ding ding." Be proud of it. This is for Jesus' sake. He is being preached loud and clear. The Father is also rejoicing in heaven. I can just imagine Him saying, "Oh he did it! Another saint who has earned persecution rewards!" If Jesus said GREAT is your reward, He meant it. This is real. You can expect it. We must step into boldness. It's the same as stepping into love. You forget about yourself and your own nice little reputation. Your aim is only to please God, to preach the gospel, and to show the love of Christ. When you do this, you are being a bright light and you are shining for the kingdom of God. You are letting God show Himself strong through you. You are doing good works. You are salty and highly seasoned, for you are the salt of the earth!

Thank you for reading this book. I pray you will meditate on the truths that you find in here and pursue God's heart like never before. I pray this book has helped to light a fire in you and given you a deep hunger for intimacy with the king. As you do this, you will never be the same, and the hunger for His presence will only grow. For only He can satisfy the great longing hidden in your heart.

Chapter Twelve – Salvation/Baptism of the Holy Spirit

You have a free choice to receive Jesus as your Lord and Savior. This is the most important decision you'll ever make!

That if thou shalt confess with thy mouth the Lord Jesus, and shalt believe in thine heart that God has raised Him from the dead, thou shalt be saved. For with the heart man believeth unto righteousness; and with the mouth confession is made unto salvation.

Romans 10:9–10

For by grace are ye saved through faith; and that not of yourselves: it is the gift of God.

Linda Patarello

Ephesians 2:8

Like a child, just believe and receive. Jesus already did all the work. It's so much easier to come to God when you understand that He is a good God who loves you no matter what. He accepts you right now as you are. You don't have to clean up first—Jesus will do that for you.

If you would like to receive Jesus Christ into your heart, all you have to do is pray this simple prayer:

Lord Jesus, I confess that you are my Lord and Savior. I believe in my heart that God raised you from the dead. By faith in your Word, I receive salvation now. I give you my life. Thank you for forgiving me of all sin, and thank you for saving me!

If you meant that with your heart, you are now saved, dear one. Remember, it has nothing to do with your feelings, only the decision you have just made. Now that you are born again, you are brand new!

> *Therefore if any man be in Christ, he is a new creature: old things are passed away; behold, all things are become new.*

2 Corinthians 5:17

Receive the Holy Spirit

When Jesus rose again to be at the right hand of the Father, He didn't want us to be alone. He told the disciples to wait—that the Father would send a comforter to be with them, a helper. As you read the Scriptures, you can see for yourself that He is from God. You can take comfort that this is a blessing. He only wants the best for us, and we need not be afraid of anything given by God, because He loves us. The Holy Spirit is a gift from God.

> *But when the Comforter is come, whom I will send unto you from the Father, even the Spirit of truth…*
>
> **John 15:26**

> *Howbeit when he, the Spirit of truth, is come, he will guide you into all truth: for he shall not speak of himself; but whatsoever he shall hear, that shall he speak: and he will shew you things to come.*
>
> **John 16:13**

> *But ye shall receive power, after that the Holy Ghost is come upon you: and ye shall be witnesses unto me both in Jerusalem, and in all.*

Salvation/Baptism of the Holy Spirit

> *Judaea, and in Samaria, and unto the uttermost part of the earth.*
>
> **Acts 1:8**

The Word explains how they were filled:

> *And they were all filled with the Holy Ghost, and began to speak with other tongues, as the Spirit gave them utterance.*
>
> **Acts 2:4**

And you must know that the Holy Spirit is still for us today because:

Linda Patarello

Jesus Christ is the same yesterday, today, and forever.
Hebrews 13:8 NKJV

If Jesus is the same, and He is one with God, then God is the same. And if God is the same, then so is His Spirit.

> *For everyone that asketh receiveth; and he that seeketh findeth; and to him that knocketh it shall be opened. If ye then...know how to give good gifts unto your children: how much more shall your heavenly Father give the Holy Spirit to them that ask Him?*
> **Luke 11:10,13**

If you would like to receive the Holy Spirit, all you have to do is ask, believe, and receive. Pray this simple prayer:

Father, I recognize my need for your power to live this new, born again life. Fill me with your Holy Spirit. By faith I receive Him right now. Thank you for baptizing me with your Holy Spirit.

It's that simple. The Holy Spirit will not come uninvited. You are now filled with God's supernatural power. Some syllables from a language you don't understand may rise up from your heart to your mouth. You may not hear anything. If so, then, by faith, speak a continuous sound out loud, but not in your own language; just make some sounds. As you do, the Holy Spirit will shape them into your prayer language, which is tongues. As you speak, you will be releasing God's power from within you by building yourself up in the Spirit.

No man understands these words, but only God. You are speaking God's mysteries, spirit to Spirit. If you don't open your mouth, nothing will come out, because it's your mouth and your tongue. The Holy Spirit will not force you to speak. You must take the first step of faith and speak, then as you do, He will help you. You may only have one word at first. That's okay. Just give it some time and practice. Just like a little child learns to speak a language, they start with a word or two at a time. Make a habit of praying in tongues. You may think, "I'm only praying one word." Maybe so, but in God's eyes, you're praying in tongues.

> *For he that speaketh in an unknown tongue speaketh not unto men, but unto God: for no man understandeth him; howbeit in the spirit he speaketh mysteries.*

1 Corinthians 14:2

> *He that speaketh in an unknown tongue edifieth himself.*

1 Corinthians 14:4

That means that you are building your spirit man up like a battery charger. You can do this whenever and wherever you like. You can pray for your loved ones. You can pray for situations in which you need wisdom. And the best part of all is that you really don't need to feel a thing. When I first received the baptism, I was in 10th grade. My Aunt Nini came over to our house in California. She started telling my mom about it and how she prays in tongues. My ears perked up. "What? Tell me about it. I want that too!" So my aunt, my mom, and I went upstairs into my mom's bedroom. My aunt

Salvation/Baptism of the Holy Spirit

prayed for me, and I spoke in tongues. I was so excited! And you know what? I didn't feel one thing! But I believed it, and I was really speaking in another language. Throughout the years, honestly there were times that I didn't speak at all for years. But it is because I didn't understand it. As I began to read the Scriptures more and was taught more about the Holy Spirit, that is when I began to pray more and more till eventually it became a habit. Now it is like breathing to me. I may be cooking or driving down the street, and I don't even realize it; I am praying in tongues. It doesn't matter if it's just a whisper; it's still tongues. Many times I sing in tongues. And I know it is going straight to God. You could say it's like having a hotline to God.

I want to thank you so much for reading this book all the way to end. I pray that the Holy Spirit will seal His Word and the revelations that you may have learned while you were reading this book. In these last days, I truly believe the highest calling for us is intimacy with God. It is our part to seek Him. It is our part to get away and spend time in His Word. It is up to us to spend time alone with Him and worship Him. No one can do this for you. God will not make you. He has already responded to you. It's your turn to answer His call and respond to His love.

Worship Him as you were made to do, in Spirit and in truth….

God is Looking for Heart Worshipers

Bibliography

Letters from a Modern Mystic by Frank C. Laubach 2007

New Testament Translation by Kenneth Wuest, Wm. B. Eerdmans Publishing 1961

Merriam Webster Online Dictionary, http://www.merriamwebster.com

The Power to Change the World by Rick Joyner Morningstar Publications 206

The Practice of the Presence of God by Brother Lawrence First Work originally published New York: FH Revel 1895

Strong's Hebrew and Greek Dictionaries.
Strong, James (1822–1894)

Electronic Edition STEP Files Copyright ©1998, Parsons Technology, Inc., all rights reserved.

About the Author

Linda Patarello is a born again Christian and a graduate of Charis Bible College in Colorado Springs. Linda is a California native and currently lives there. She has served as a worship leader for many years, while also writing music as well as books. She believes that the highest calling is to worship the "Giver of All Gifts". Intimacy and a relationship with God as our Father is a priority that she loves to share with others. Awakening to the acceptance of being in God's family and that we are called to be His mature sons is the message that she believes is vital in this day.

For more information or to contact the author, write to:

Heaven's Treasures

Linda Patarello

PO Box 1543

Anaheim, CA 92815   www.heavenstreasures.org

Other books by Linda Patarello

The Father Loves

How to Meditate on the Living Word

Song of Solomon

Purchase these books on www.heavenstreasures.org
and also on Amazon.

God is Looking for Heart Worshipers